Artist's Library Series

Steps to Success in Watercolor

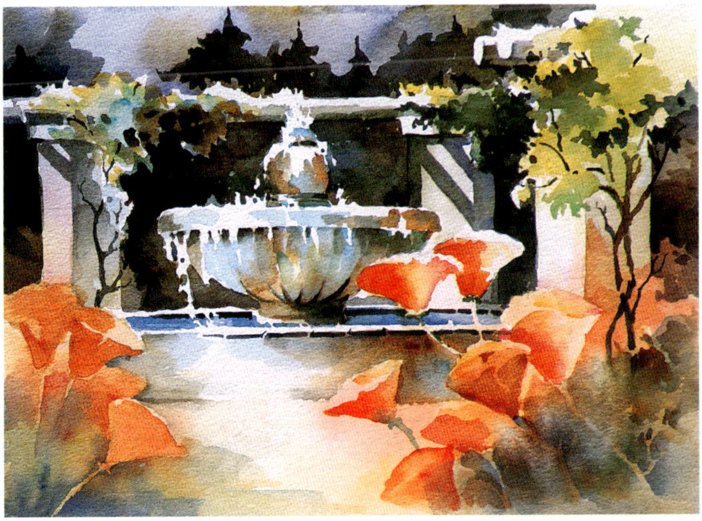

by Brenda Swenson

Brenda would like to thank her students and her fellow artists for filling her life with joy, inspiration, and endless gratitude.

Walter Foster Publishing, Inc.
23062 La Cadena Drive
Laguna Hills, CA 92653
www.walterfoster.com

Contents

The Value of Planning

I often see artists get excited about painting—so excited that they rush right in without any preparation. Later I listen to the their list of regrets: "If only I had corrected my drawing, saved some whites, varied shapes, had better values. . . ." Preparation is the smart artist's insurance policy—it's a small-scale investment of your time to ensure that your effort, energy, and hopes aren't wasted in the long run. To plan for success, all you need to do is think before you paint!

Having a plan won't take the joy out of painting; instead it will make it more enjoyable. A plan allows you to walk through the painting in your mind, much like rehearsing. Wouldn't you feel better getting up and speaking in front of an audience if you had a dry run of the material first? Painting takes the same kind of practice. Even a little bit of preparation will help you jump into painting with confidence in your heart!

Once I understood the value of planning my paintings, my work changed in quality, and success became a common occurrence. You can experience that same sense of accomplishment. In this book, I'm going to share with you eight principles that will help you strengthen your painting skills. In each section, I'll focus on one step of preparation. With each new lesson, you'll build a stronger understanding of what makes a painting work. And when you reach the final project, you'll discover how to tie all the principles together to complete a successful watercolor painting, step by step!

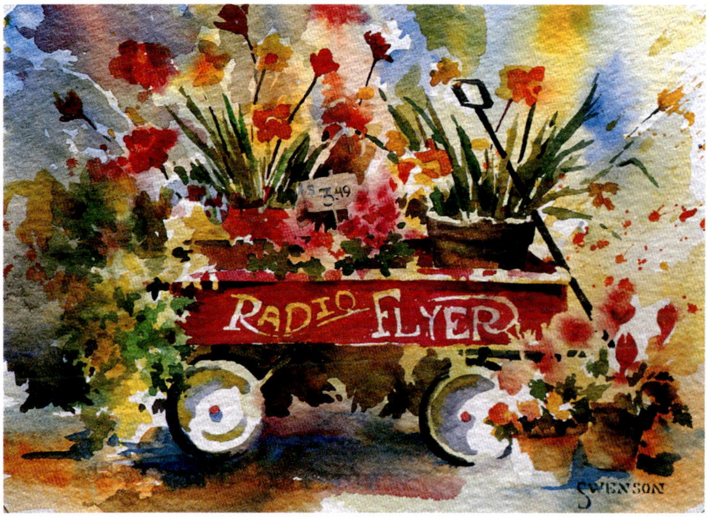

Tools and Materials

Art materials don't come in "one size fits all." As an artist, you'll develop preferences for specific colors, palettes, papers, and even pens! But first you'll need to take the time to get to know your options. Quality matters—but what matters more is your comfort level. Here I've summarized my "must have" items. Feel free to use these pages as a guide when selecting your own supplies—but always consider your own personal preferences.

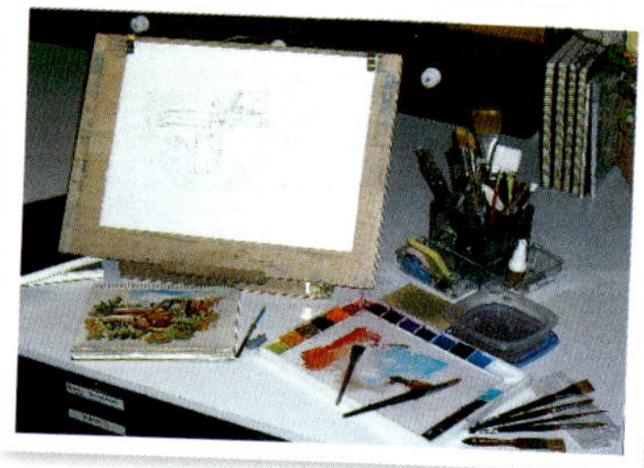

Workspace Equip your work area with a chair, music, or whatever makes you feel comfortable and inspired. For uninterrupted workflow, keep your supplies organized and close at hand. For lighting, a window that lets in natural light is ideal, but artificial light is necessary for gray days or nighttime painting sessions.

Paint

Watercolors are available in tubes, pans, or cakes. I prefer tubes because they make it easy to squeeze out large quantities of color, but you may find another type suits you best. Whatever you choose, splurge on artist-grade paints. Student-grade colors lack brilliance, transparency, and permanence—they're not intended for you, the artist! Invest in quality and you'll see the difference in your artwork.

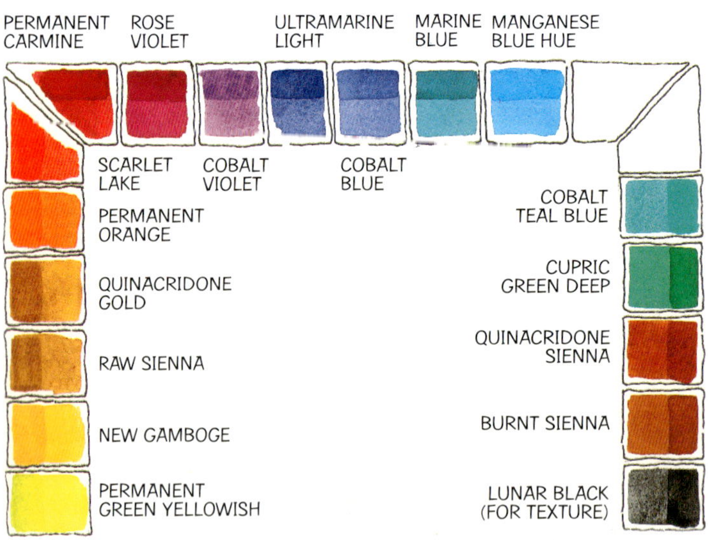

◀ **Color Palette** You'll rarely use every color you have available for a painting, but it's nice to have a range of choices. For ease of use, I arrange my palette from warm (yellows and reds) to cool (blues and greens).

▼ **Mixing Palette** Folding metal palettes are nice for painting on the go because the lid provides room for mixing washes while also allowing portability.

Mixing Palettes

"Palette" can refer both to an artist's selection of colors and the container used to hold those paints. When considering the second type of palette, be sure to look for one with a large area to mix your washes and deep wells to hold an ample quantity of each color so you won't need to interrupt your workflow to refill empty wells. I prefer a plastic palette with 20 wells, room for a variety of colors. When you add paint to your palette, don't be afraid to fill the wells: If your paint dries, all it takes is a little water to revive it.

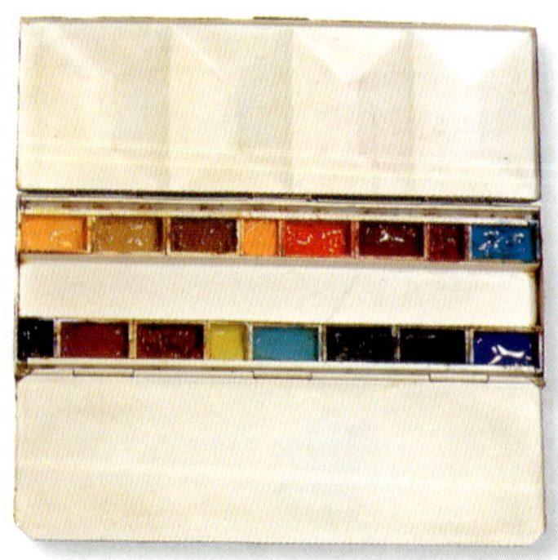

Paintbrushes

Paintbrushes are made with either natural (animal) or synthetic hair. The most expensive watercolor brushes are natural-hair sables, which can come with a shocking price tag. But I leave the small animals alone—the quality of synthetic-hair brushes has improved greatly over the years, and I couldn't be more pleased with the results. Synthetic brushes fit my needs just fine.

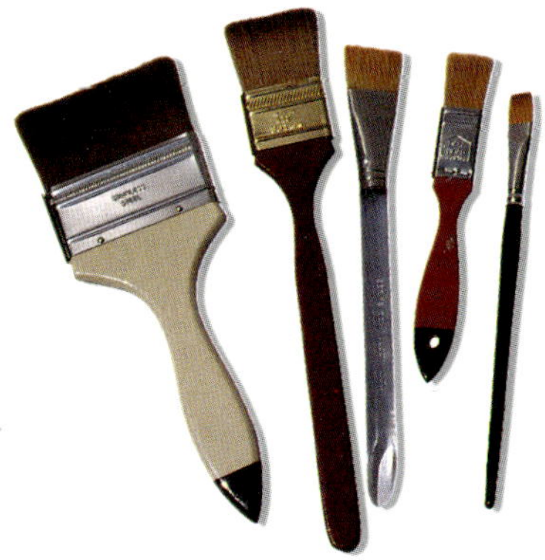

▲ **Flat Brushes** Flat brushes are ideal for covering large areas of a painting. Keep them in a range of sizes, from 1/4" to 1-1/2"—plus an extra-large wash brush!

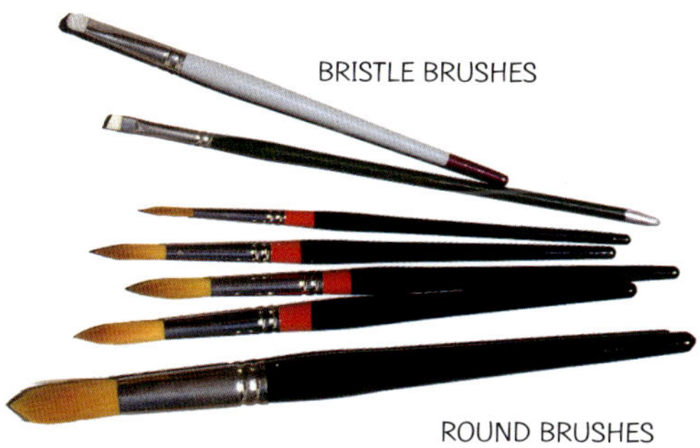

◀ **Other Brushes** Invest in a variety of round brushes so you'll have an appropriate size for any occasion. You also may want a couple of stiff oil-painting bristle brushes for techniques like lifting out (see page 12).

Drawing Tools

Painters need to become just as familiar with their pencil and pen as they are with their paintbrush! I prefer a 2B or a 4B pencil for drawing on watercolor paper, and I use a 4B or a 6B for creating value studies (see page 20). I also use markers with brush tips or dual tips; keep a variety of colors on hand for sketching and planning paintings. And water-soluble pens and markers are wonderful for value studies because the color easily moves with a damp brush.

Drawing Implements In addition to pencils, I have an assortment of pens that I use when working out designs or arrangements in a sketchbook. And no artist is equipped without an eraser! Kneaded erasers are great for lifting out lights in value studies or for working on delicate paper. Vinyl erasers are soft and won't tear or stain your paper.

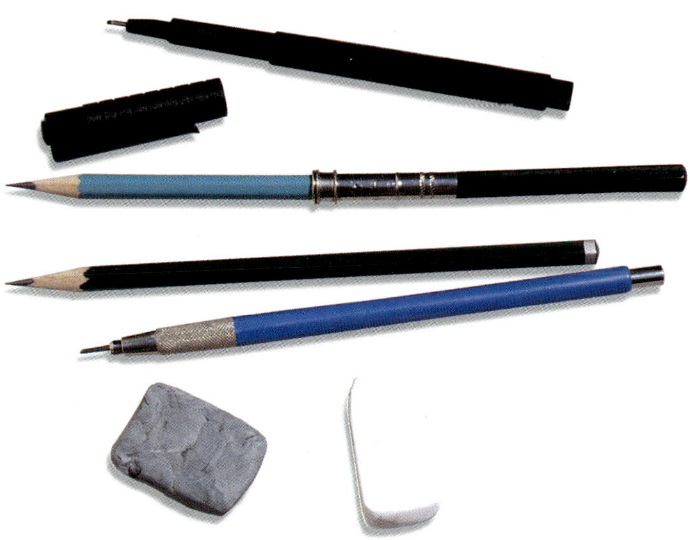

Papers

Watercolor papers come in different qualities, thicknesses, and textures. Student-grade paper is fine for practicing brushstrokes or washes—but as its surface can be unmanageable even after you've mastered watercolor, it's best to stick with higher-grade papers. The thickness of watercolor paper is indicated by its weight—the higher the number, the thicker the paper. The standard used by the majority of artists is professional-quality 140 lb or heavier. I use a good quality, 140 lb, 100% rag paper, and I prefer a cold-pressed texture (see caption at right).

Paper Surfaces Watercolor papers can have one of three surface textures: Hot-press (left), cold-press (center), and rough (right). The differences among them are visible but become even more obvious when paint is applied to the paper.

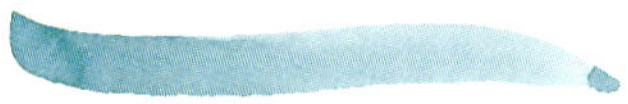

Smooth Hot-pressed watercolor paper has a fine-grain surface, with almost no texture.

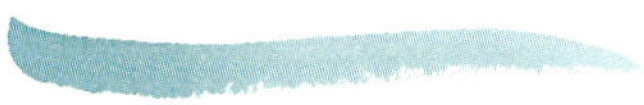

Medium Cold-pressed watercolor paper has a slightly textured surface.

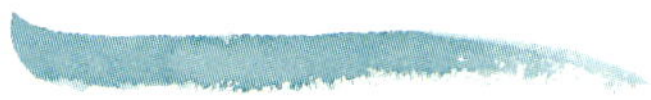

Rough Rough watercolor paper has a prominent *tooth,* or textured surface.

Sketchbooks

A sketchbook can be useful for working out compositions, value studies, and colors for a painting. Keep a lot of notes next to your sketches, and you'll have a valuable resource you can refer to time and time again. For more about using a sketchbook with watercolor, see my book *Keeping a Watercolor Sketchbook* (AL46) in Walter Foster's Artist's Library Series.

I'm not fond of stretching watercolor paper, so I rarely do! If a painting warps, flatten it when you're finished painting. Relax the paper by moistening the back with a damp sponge. Then place a large towel, a piece of plywood, and a few heavy books on top. By morning, you'll have a flat painting!

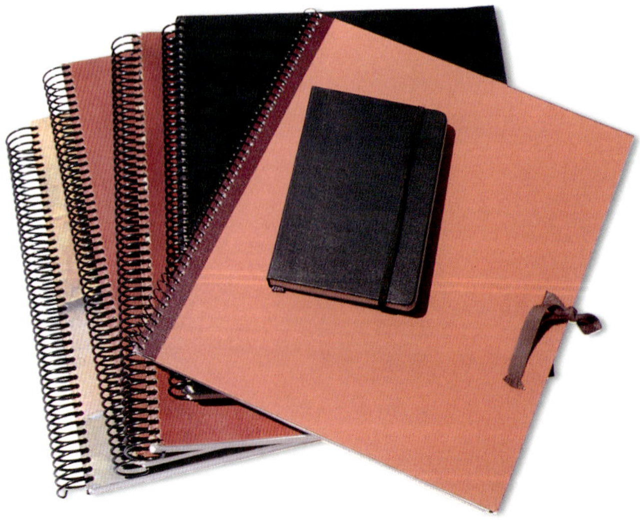

◀ **Sketchbook Choices** Always look for sketchbooks that are spiral-bound with pages that are dense enough to handle multiple washes of color without warping or bleeding through.

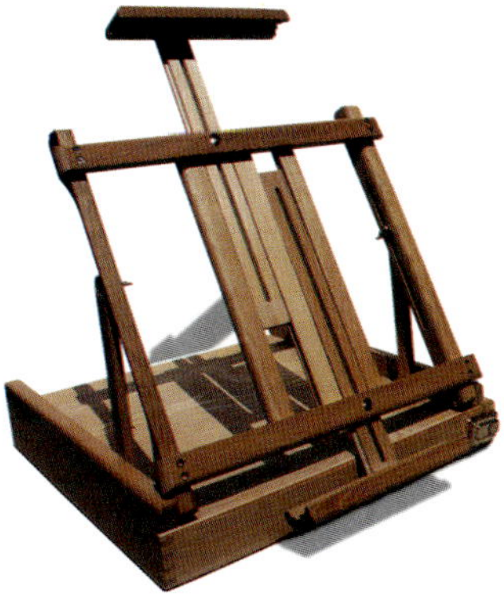

Supports

Just like the term palette, "support" has two meanings to artists. Some artists call their paper or other painting surface the "support." But I think of a support as the object that holds your paper in place as you paint. Easels or boards with binder clips both make good supports. I switch between the two depending on my needs. In fact, when I'm painting outdoors, I use a hybrid: a support that my husband created with an acrylic surface attached to a tripod easel base.

▲ **Easel** Easels are a nice tool for watercolorists because they allow you to angle the paper from flat to vertical, so washes can run down the page instead of pooling. A small easel like this one is perfect for working in the studio.

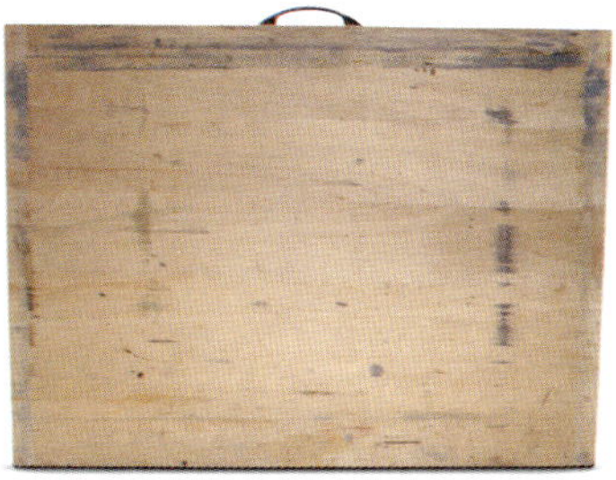

◀ **Board Support** A large (approximately 18" x 24") lightweight wood board is another support option. The large surface isn't the only benefit—you can attach binder clips to the board, providing an ideal way to hold your paper in place as you work.

Extras

There are a few other items you'll want to have on hand before you begin painting: towels for cleanup, sponges—both for painting and for sopping up extra water, water containers for rinsing brushes and adding water to your paints, and a spray bottle for misting your paints to keep them moist.

▶ **Additional Items** You'll be surprised at how many household items double as painting tools! Sponges, paper towels, binder clips, and spray bottles are just a few things you might use. Later you may even want to raid your kitchen for plastic wrap (see page 13).

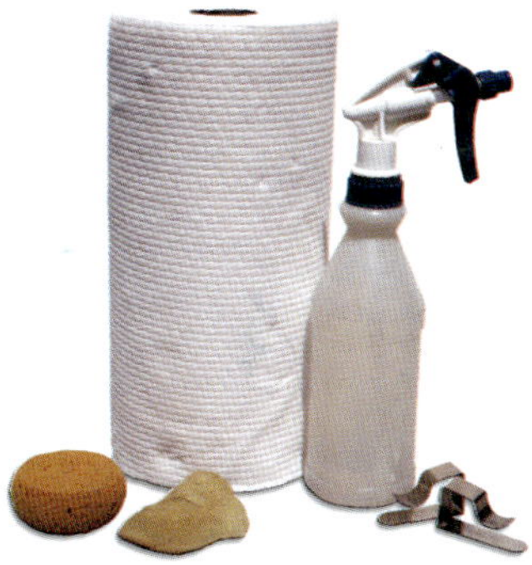

The Computer As a Tool

In this modern age, most of us have digital cameras and computers. If you become familiar with your camera's editing program, you can use it as an artist's tool too. Editing, cropping, zooming in, and changing your photos to grayscale (black and white) to help you see values are just a few of the ways the computer can assist you in planning your paintings. If you have a scanner, you can even test out potential layouts and color palettes!

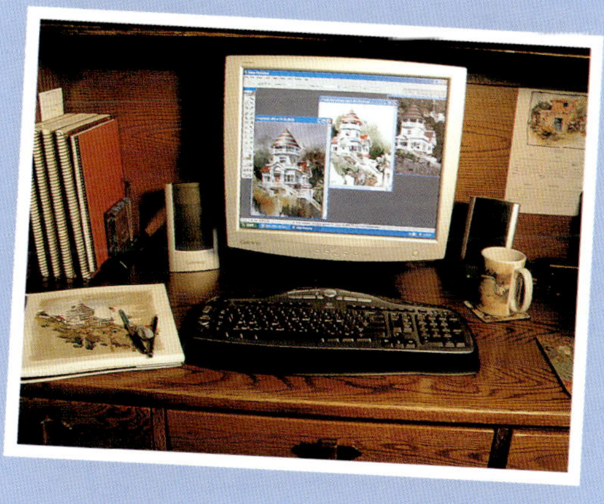

Color Basics

When you first start working in watercolor, the notion that you have to understand color theory on top of everything else can be really daunting! But color is extremely important to painting, so try to learn as much as you can about it. After some experience, color will feel natural and instinctive to you. In the meantime, don't let yourself become overwhelmed—just stick with it! The payoff you'll see in your finished paintings makes it worthwhile.

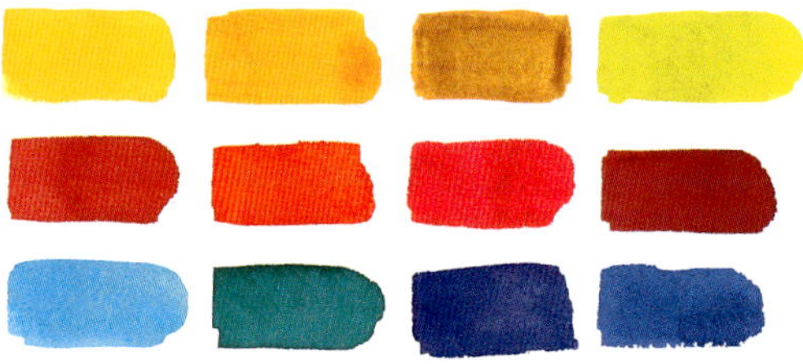

Hue Versus Color The terms "color" and "hue" are sometimes used interchangeably, but they're really different things. Each color comes in a variety of different hues. The swatches above show a sampling of the hues contained within each primary color.

Color Language

Artists have their own language to describe the quality or character of color. Three of the most important terms are hue, value, and intensity. *Hue* both names a variation within a color and describes similar colors. For example, Prussian, ultramarine, and cerulean are hues of blue—and they're also close in hue. *Value* refers to the lightness or darkness of a color. When you describe a color as pale, light, or dark, you're referring to its value. *Intensity* describes saturation. It refers to the brilliance or relative strength of a color.

Color Wheel

Color wheels demonstrate relationships among colors, such as *primary colors* (which can't be created by mixing), *secondary colors* (mixes of two primaries), and *tertiary colors* (mixes of a primary and a secondary). Colors near one another on the wheel are *analogous;* they create a sense of harmony when used together. Colors opposite each other on the wheel are *complementary*; they neutralize each other when mixed, and they create dramatic contrasts when placed next to each other.

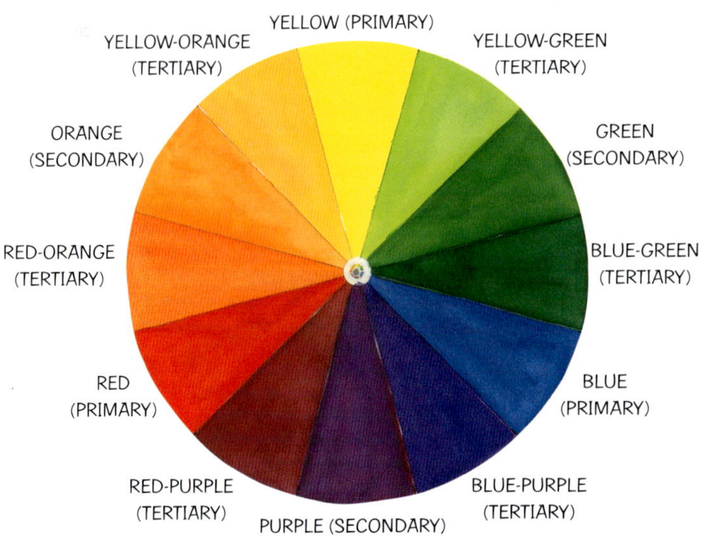

Personalizing the Color Wheel The color wheel shown here demonstrates the relationships among the colors from my palette specifically. You should make a color wheel using the colors you plan to paint with to learn the unique ways your choices interact.

Color Mixing

It's rare to find an exact match for your artistic vision directly out of a tube—color, after all, is a very personal thing! And manufactured colors rarely represent natural objects without a little manipulation. So artists rely on color mixing to produce the various hues that make up their paintings.

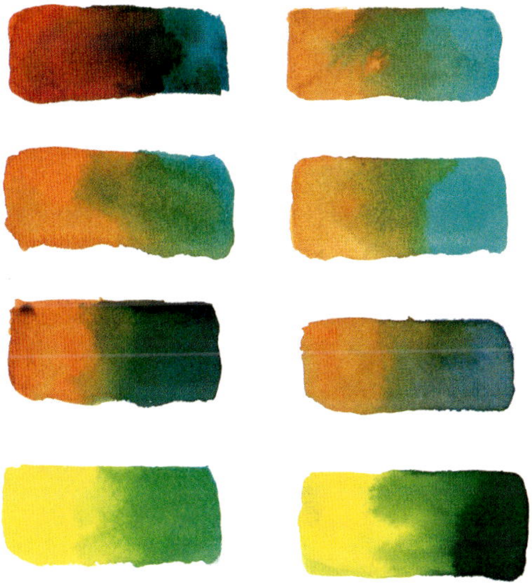

Mixing Greens

There was a time when I didn't have any green paints in my palette. Even with the one green I use now (cupric green deep), I still mix blues and yellows to create the greens for my paintings. You can mix richer, more varied, and more natural greens than you can find in a tube.

◀ **Discover Your Options** Here are a few examples of the way the blues and yellows from my palette combine to create rich, expressive greens. Experiment with your own selection of paint colors to see what new colors you can produce.

Mixing Neutrals

Neutral colors don't get much glory, but they're an important part of any painting. Black and gray paints straight from a tube can be dull and flat, but they're rarely flat when mixed from color complements—and glowing, vibrant neutrals can change the appearance of your entire painting! Play with complementary colors to see the beautiful combinations they can make.

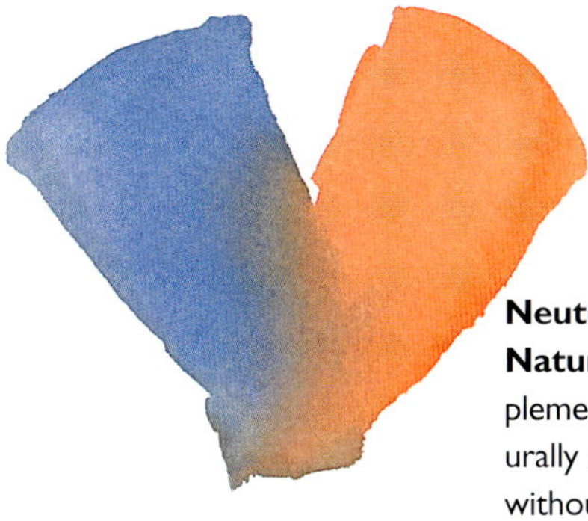

Neutralizing Naturally Complement blue naturally dulls orange without affecting its vibrancy.

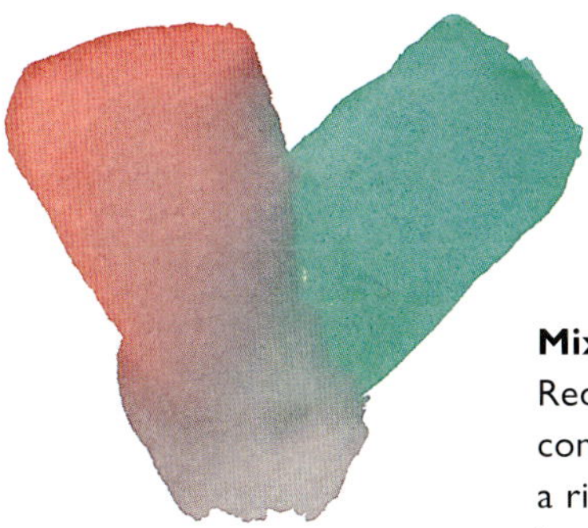

Mixing Gray Red and green combine to make a rich, natural-looking gray.

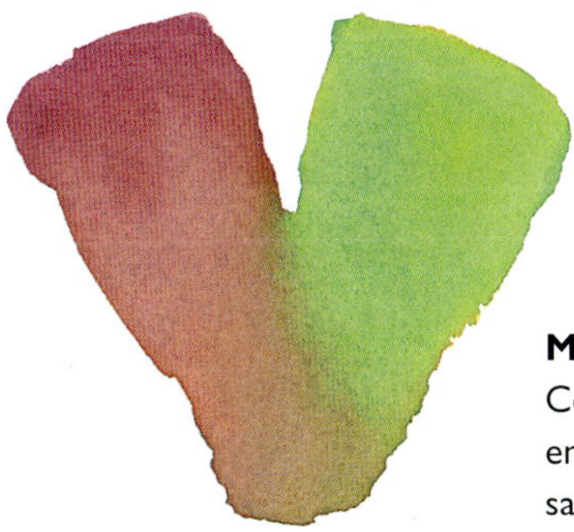

Mixing It Up Combine different hues of the same complementary colors for variation.

Mixing Techniques

There are three main ways to mix watercolor; each is unique and has its own applications and charm! For uniform color, you can mix paints directly on the palette. If you prefer a more subtle effect, try *glazing*—applying a thin wash of paint over an already-dry color. Because watercolor is transparent, you see through each application of color, and layers of color appear to blend visually. For a less predictable result, try mixing your color on the paper—wet paint touched into wet paint. It's difficult to control the way the colors merge and blend with this method, but it can produce surprising and exciting results. An understanding of how to handle these techniques will provide you with an even greater range of colors.

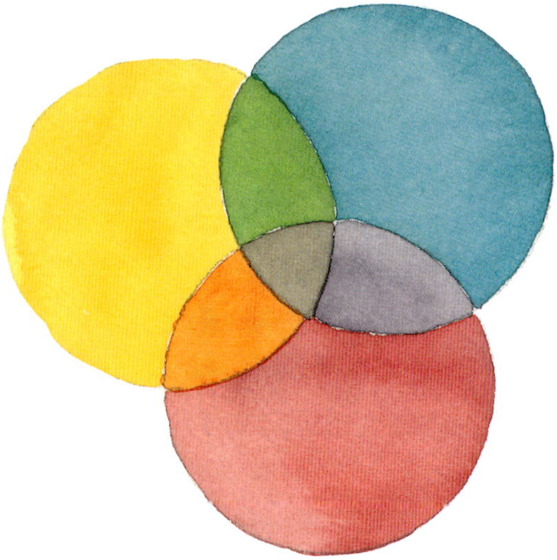

◀ **Mixing on the Palette** New gamboge, permanent carmine, and marine blue create a distinct, well-defined hue when mixed on the palette. (The pure colors are on the outer edges, and the mix is created where the colors overlap.) Mixing on the palette produces the most consistent, even results.

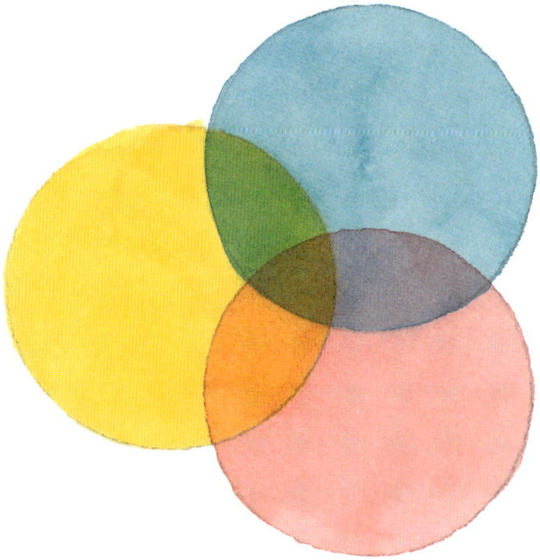

▶ **Mixing by Glazing** When the same colors are glazed, the effect is more subtle. All the original colors are still apparent in the final mix, and the visible variation gives your color mixes interest.

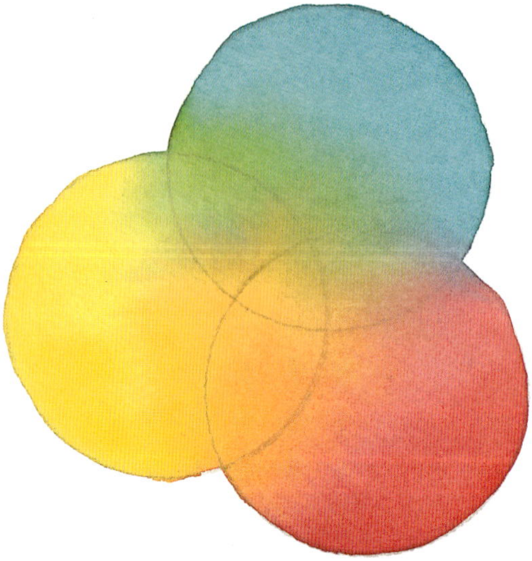

◀ **Mixing Wet into Wet** If you apply a wet color next to another wet color, the effect is quite different. The two colors blend and merge with soft irregularity. These blends can be difficult to control, but the unpredictable mix may be just what you need!

Transparency

Watercolor is a transparent medium, but the colors vary in their degree of transparency. (Most manufacturers identify the transparency of each of their colors on the tubes or on color charts.) More transparent colors are excellent for working in layered washes or glazes—the transparent washes can create glittering qualities as they mix before your eyes, like thin layers of colored glass. Opaque colors are more solid, making them good for initial washes or accents in a painting. But using an opaque color on top of other washes can result in a chalky appearance, muddying up underlying colors.

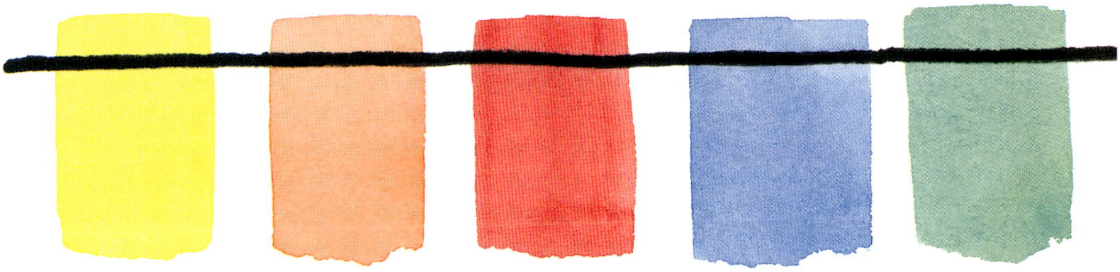

Testing Transparency You can easily check to see if a color is transparent. First use a permanent black marker or waterproof ink to draw a heavy line across a small scrap of watercolor paper. Then apply a wash of the color over the black line. Does the paint appear to sink below the line? If so, it's transparent!

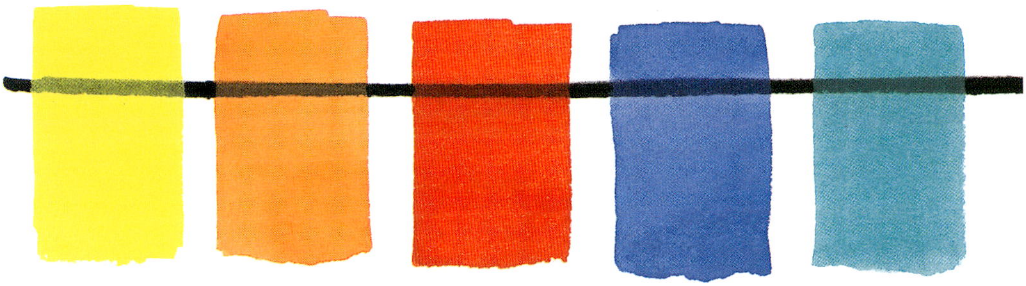

Testing Opacity If the paint sits on top of the black line (as it does with these examples), the paint is opaque. With opaque paints, the line looks chalky. (Keep in mind that any paint can become transparent if diluted with enough water—but it might lack the desired color intensity.)

Granulation

Certain watercolor pigments granulate—in other words, the pigments separate from the binder and settle into the valleys of textured watercolor paper, producing a grainy, mottled effect. Incorporating granulating colors is a wonderful way to bring interest and texture to what could be a dull area of a painting. And mixing granulating and non-granulating colors together can also create rich visual textures.

Granulation is a natural property of pigments such as cerulean blue, French ultramarine blue, manganese blue hue, and raw sienna. Rock the paper back and forth to encourage pigment to settle.

Painting Basics

There are as many different approaches to painting as there are artists, but there are a few nuts-and-bolts methods, techniques, and even designs that all artists include in their paintings. The basics are covered here—from simple washes to special effects and design principles. Get to know these building blocks, and then have fun adjusting them as you please to suit your own style.

Basic Techniques

◀ **Flat Wash** The flat wash is the most basic of all watercolor techniques. Slant your paper at a slight angle, load a flat brush with plenty of paint, and—starting at the top of the paper—slowly draw the brush across the width of the paper, letting a "bead" of paint accumulate at the bottom of the stroke. Then load your brush with more paint to make another horizontal stroke under the first, picking up the "bead" from the first pass with the edge of your brush. Repeat.

▶ **Graded Wash** When you want smooth transitions from dark to light—such as for open skies—a graded wash is the answer. First wet the paper with a large brush or sponge and clean water. Then apply the first stroke of color exactly as you would for a flat wash. Now rinse your brush and apply another stroke, slightly overlapping the first stroke. You'll pick up color from the original stroke, but it will be a little lighter in value. Keep rinsing your brush after each stroke to further dilute the wash as you move down the paper.

Special Techniques

Texture can add interest and excitement to a subject. Special techniques can be just the thing to create the appearance of ice, rust, rocks, and more. But use them conservatively so they don't overwhelm.

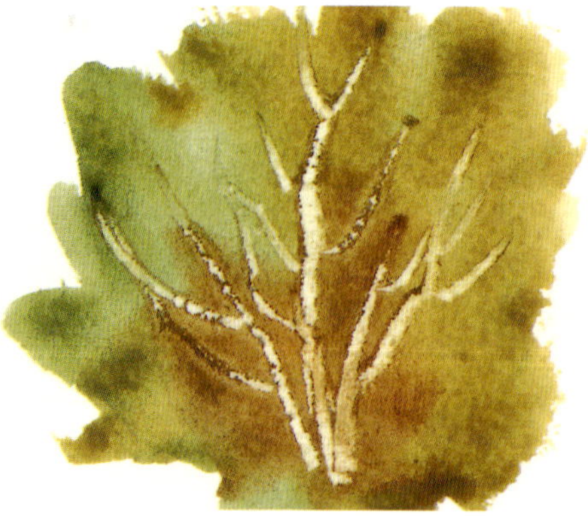

Scraping Out To remove a thin line of color, wait until the wet paint develops a matte shine. Then use the chiseled end of a brush or a palette knife to gently scrape across the paper's surface.

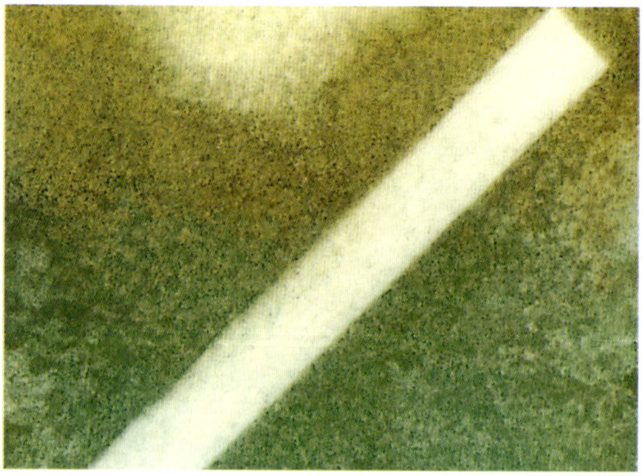

Lifting Out Once paint is dry, you can lift out color to create highlights or correct mistakes. Gently agitate the paint with a stiff, damp bristle brush; then blot the lifted color with a paper towel.

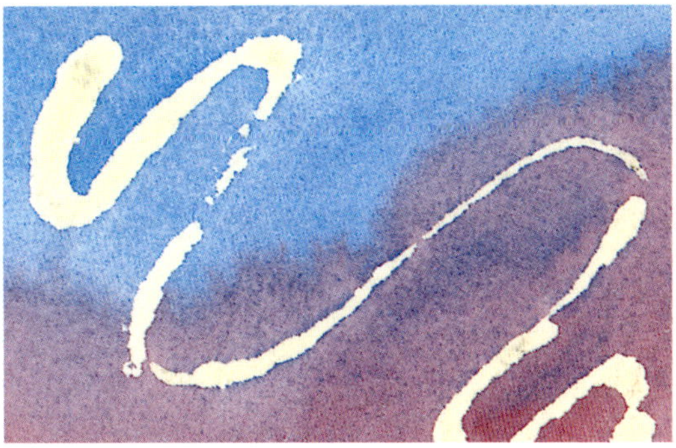

◀ **Masking Fluid** Masking fluid dries to become a rubbery substance that repels paint. This product acts as a barrier, protecting whites by blocking them from new applications of paint. Masking can be helpful when painting around an object that might otherwise disrupt a wash. When the paint dries, you can gently rub off the mask. (Don't use a good brush to apply the mask, as it can ruin bristles. Protect your brush by applying a small amount of liquid soap to the bristles before use, and clean your brush immediately after.)

▶ **Spatter** This technique creates a spray of color. Some artists incorporate fine spatter for sandy or coarse textures. Others use bold spatter effects, as shown here. Use a piece of scrap paper to shield any area of your painting you want to protect. Load a soft brush with paint, then tap the handle against your other hand to release color. A little spatter goes a long way—rein yourself in unless you want to achieve a Jackson Pollock-style result.

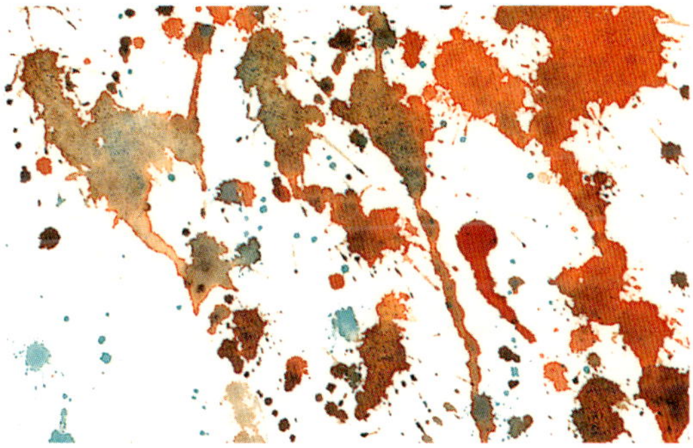

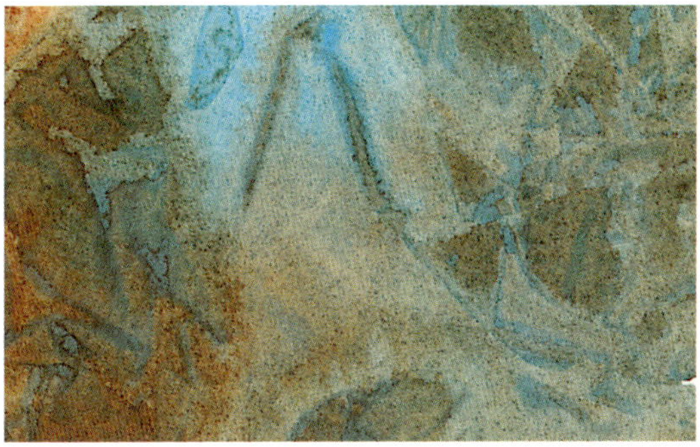

◀ **Plastic Wrap** You can use plastic wrap to create an irregular textured impression in your painting. The best approach is to crumple the plastic wrap and press it into the paint while it is still shiny. Then put a small book or another lightweight item on top of the wrap to hold it in place until the paint is nearly dry. You'll enjoy the unique visual texture this technique produces!

▶ **Water** Yes, watercolor is water-based, but typically the water is mixed into the paint rather than splashed on it. Sprinkling or spraying water onto a damp section of paint is a very simple way to create an interesting texture. The effect is a forced (and thus more controlled) bloom, similar to what can be achieved with salt. Just be sure to wait until your paper has a matte shine before spritzing!

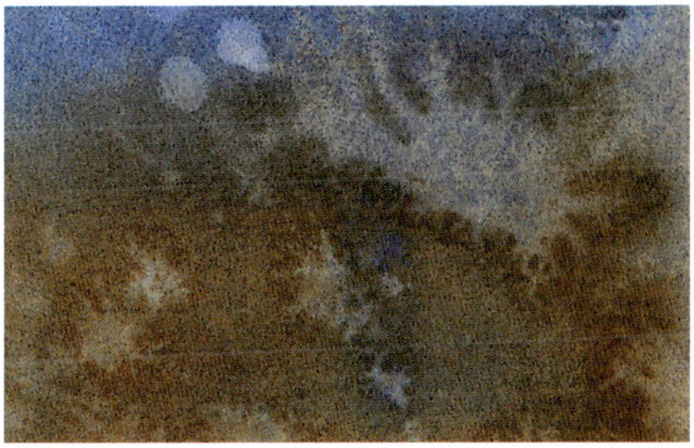

Many artists use salt to create texture, and the effects can be great. But I think that salt is best for seasoning food. My unease comes from salt's corrosive nature. If it can deteriorate metal, do you really want to put it on your painting? Sprinkling water offers a close enough texture substitute for me.

Composition

Composition refers to the organization, arrangement, and combination of objects within the frame of a space—or in this case, within the borders of a painting. All works of art should have an order of some sort, whether balanced and symmetrical or deliberately chaotic and seemingly random. The composition methods discussed here are classics you will see time and time again—and it's hard to go wrong when you base your composition on one of these perennial favorites.

▶ **Grouped Mass** In this composition, several items in one area create unity. The trick to this is establishing one element as clearly dominant, then supporting it with the other elements.

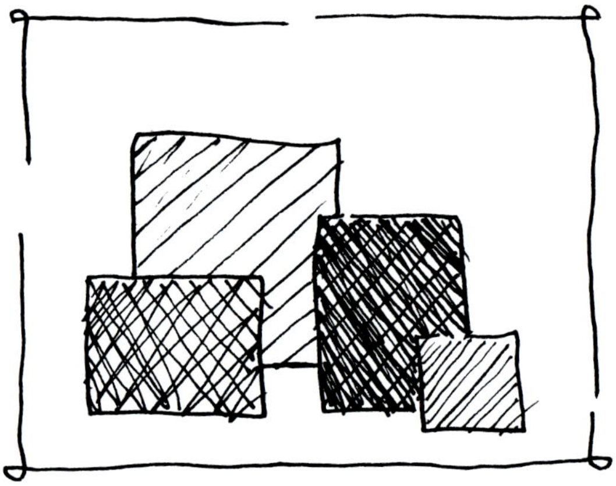

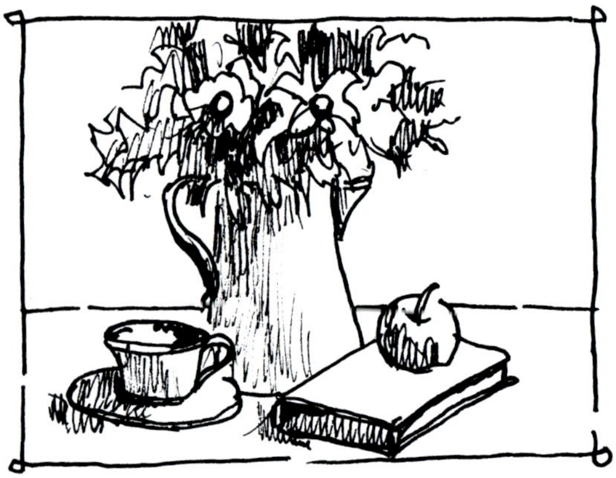

◀ **Size Dominance** The dominant element in a grouped mass should be larger than the other items. Here the pitcher of flowers is clearly dominant.

Color Dominance Size isn't the only way to establish dominance. The dominant object can also be set apart through color, texture, or value difference. Here your eye is immediately drawn to the white pitcher because of its stark contrast to the dark background.

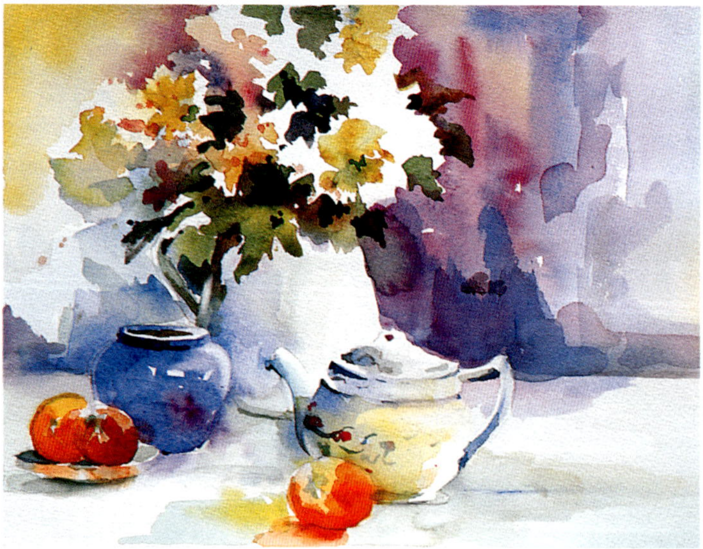

"The art of being wise is the art of knowing what to overlook."
–William James

Steelyard The steelyard is named after a weighing mechanism similar to a balance scale. Visualize this composition as a seesaw where a bar rests on a support to balance one heavy object and one light object. The larger object rests on the shortest end of the bar, nearer the support. The smaller one rests on the long end. For balance, both objects should have a similar color and/or value. In this seascape scene, the "heavy" lighthouse is complemented by the "light" sailboat. For the sake of balance, the lighthouse is located just to the left of center, whereas the sailboat is placed farther in the distance, away from the central "support" of the imaginary scale.

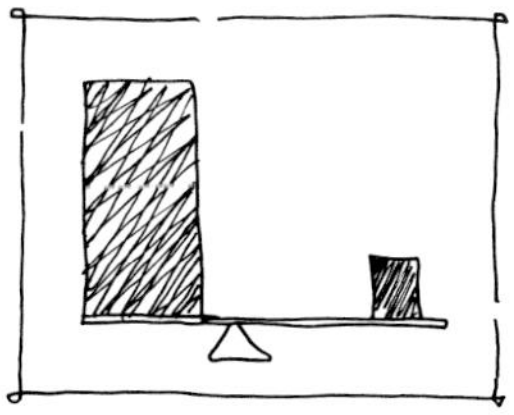

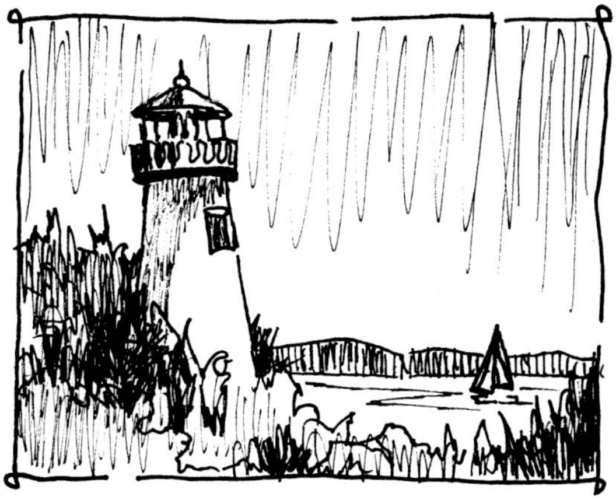

Cruciform The cruciform is a cross created when dominant vertical and horizontal shapes intersect. Your center of interest sits where these two shapes converge. The key to making this composition work is placing the intersection off center, both vertically and horizontally. Keeping the corners of the subject simple also helps frame the dominant shapes. In the simple scene at right, the truck provides a very clear vertical stroke of value, which is extended by the dark foliage placed below it. The horizontal stroke of the truck is too short to balance the cruciform—but a little extra foliage is all that is needed to extend the value across the page for a solid composition.

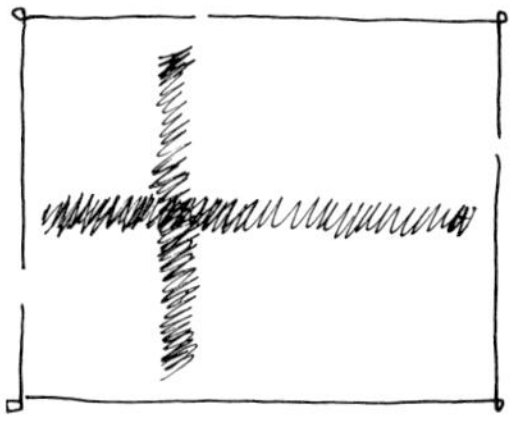

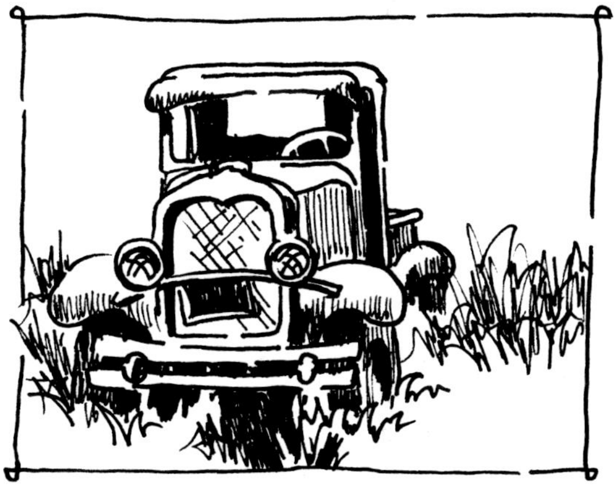

S Curve The visual curve of this format guides the eye through a painting with a slow, graceful movement. Frequently, you'll see this composition used to direct the viewer's eye through a painting, from the foreground, into the middle ground, and finally into the distance. For this reason, the S curve is a popular composition for landscapes like the one at right. The eye follows the S-shaped road all the way through the composition, starting in the foreground and meandering through the foliage before finally resting on the building and trees located in the background of the scene.

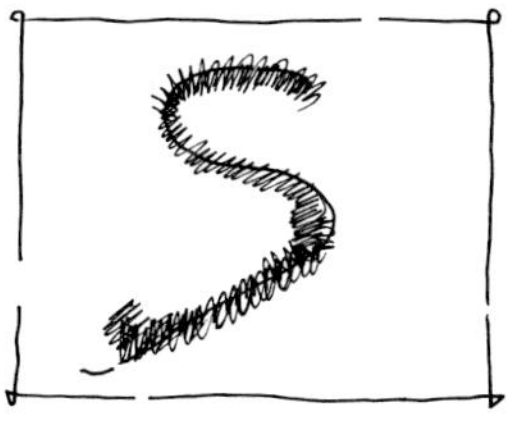

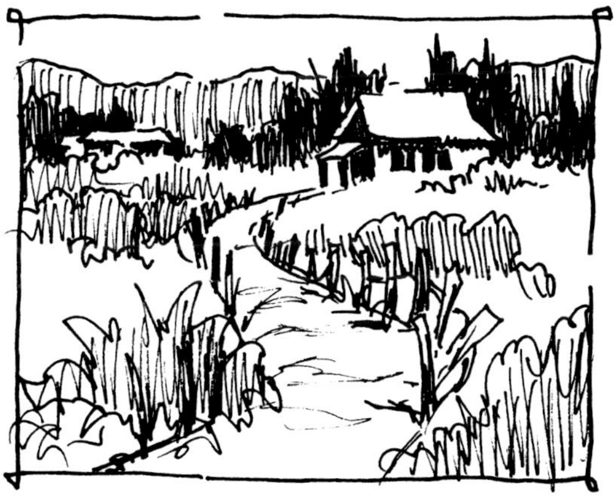

Step One: Compose the Elements

One of the most exciting aspects of being an artist is being able to create what doesn't exist! Artists aren't required to replicate exactly what they see. Rather than being bound by your references, think of them as nothing more than ingredients. It's up to you, the artist, to determine the combination, using your imagination and your experience to combine the raw materials in a creative way. Use your artistic freedom (also called "artistic license") to rearrange the elements, exclude extraneous details, combine information from multiple sources, and determine the subject's most flattering format.

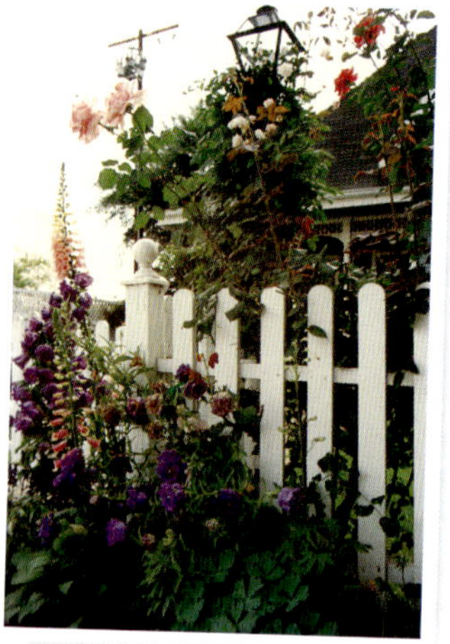

Be Resourceful Carry a camera or a sketchbook with you to collect ingredients for your paintings. You never know when you'll need colorful flowers to spice up a bland subject!

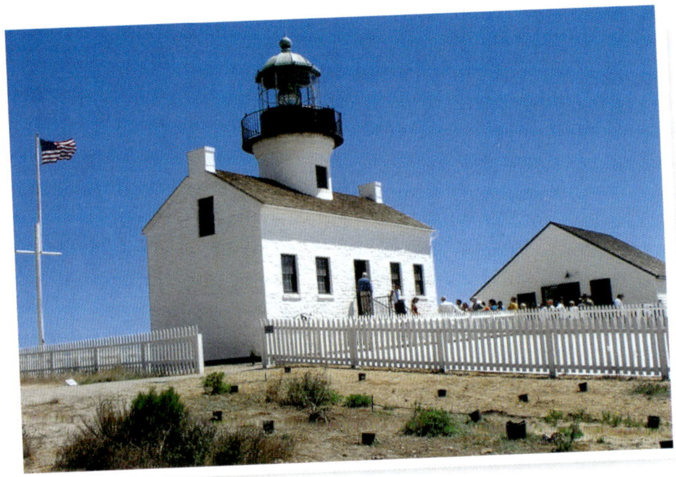

Use Your Imagination A photo can be a springboard for your imagination. The camera doesn't have a brain—so use *yours* to assess what the camera records. Will this image make a good painting? Not as it stands—but it's a good beginning.

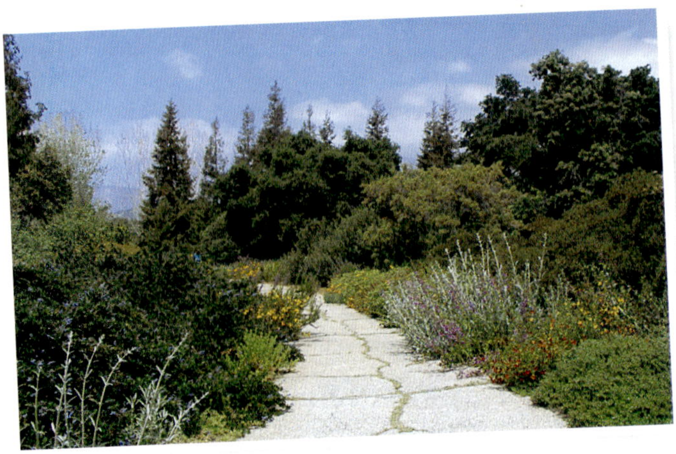

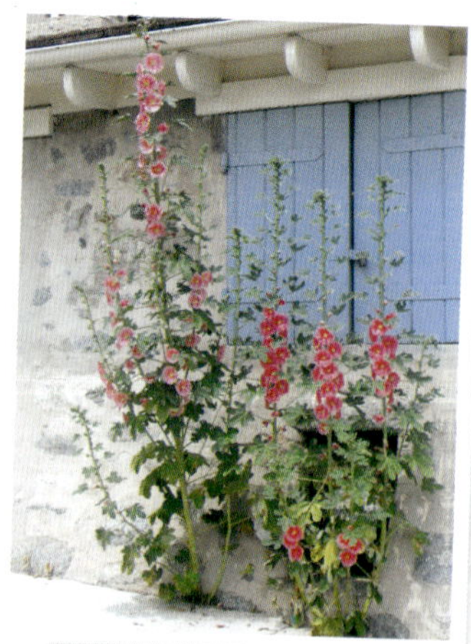

Record Ideas and Inspiration If any aspect of a scene catches your interest, it's worth recording. Remember: The camera records every detail, but the artist decides which details are important.

Elements

When you've selected a set of four or five elements you think will combine well, the next step is to arrange them. First sketch the elements at the top of your paper. (This will help you isolate and simplify them in your mind.) Then choose at least three of the elements and sketch them in a simple arrangement. The elements are not like pieces of a puzzle because they can be arranged and rearranged in any number of combinations—you can even move them into different planes of the drawing, such as from the foreground into the distance! It's common to try at least three different arrangements before you start to feel an understanding for the elements. If you sketch with a pen, you'll focus on making new arrangements as opposed to correcting previous ones!

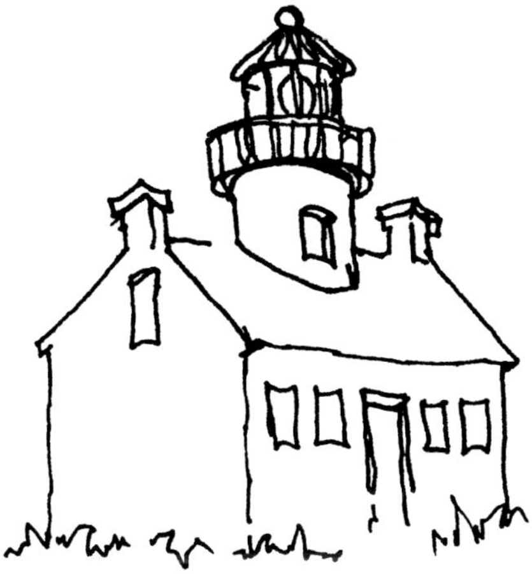

LIGHTHOUSE

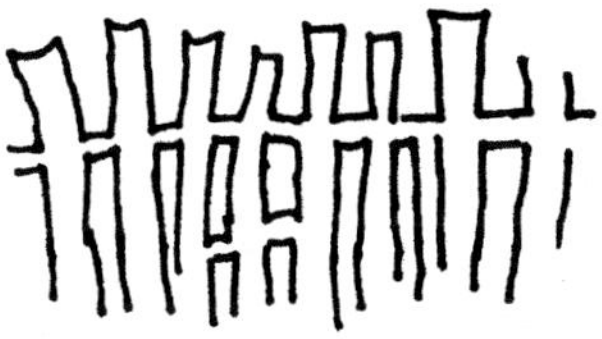

FENCE

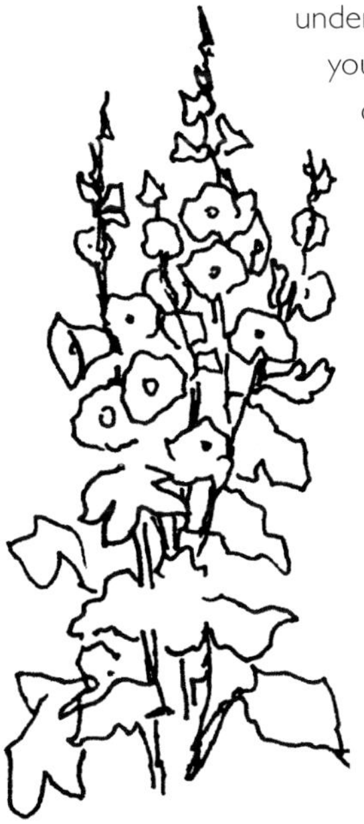

HOLLYHOCKS

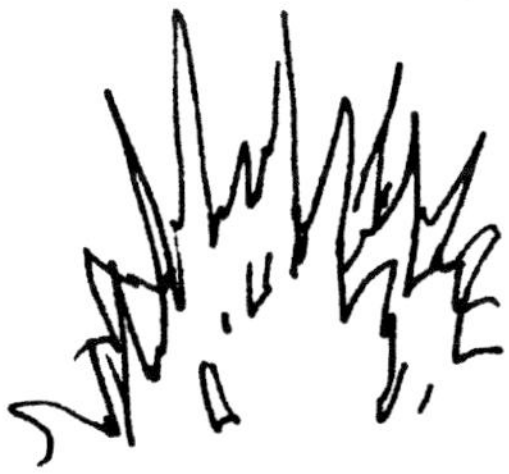

SHRUBS

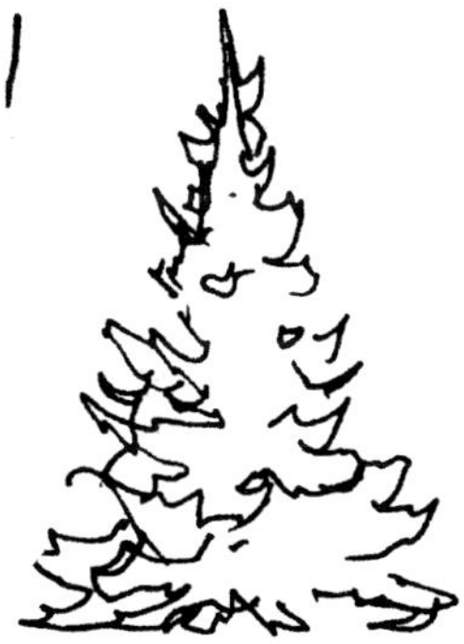

TREES

Formats

When you're trying to fit a scene into a predetermined box, you're less likely to feel free to let the image evolve. So don't start thinking about the best format for a painting until after you've drawn the elements together. The four most common formats are landscape, portrait, square, and panorama.

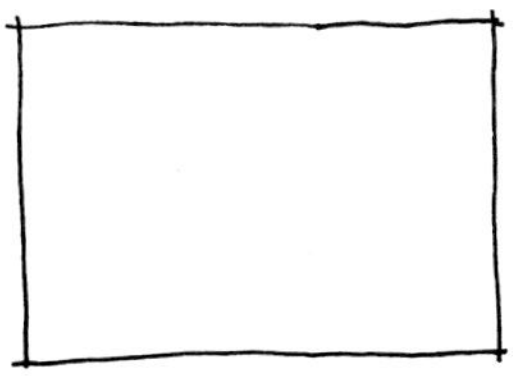

LANDSCAPE

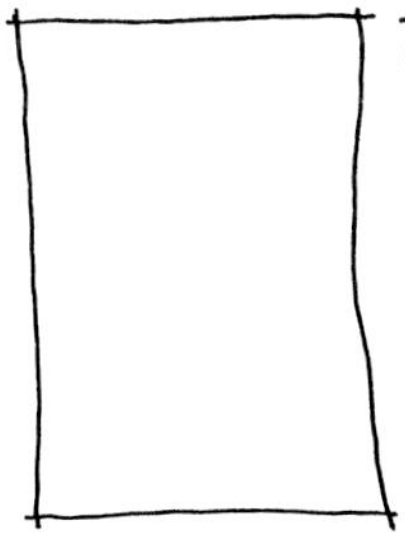

PORTRAIT

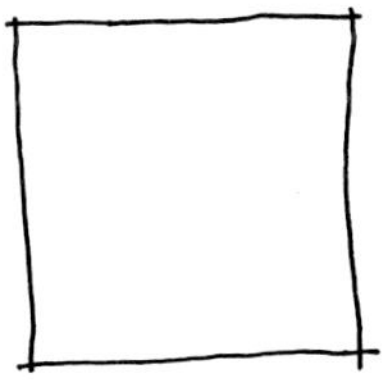

SQUARE

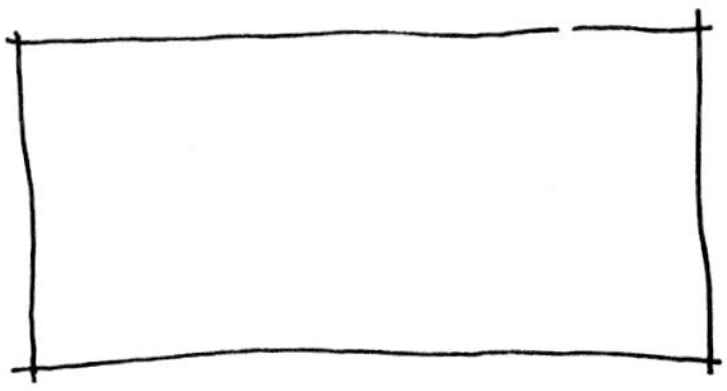

PANORAMA

Rearranging Elements

Now sketch the elements of the scene again, this time trying them out in several different formats. It typically takes me about four attempts to get a good feeling for the scene and my choices—even in cases when I'm happy with my first arrangement. No matter how many years you've been painting, never skip this important step.

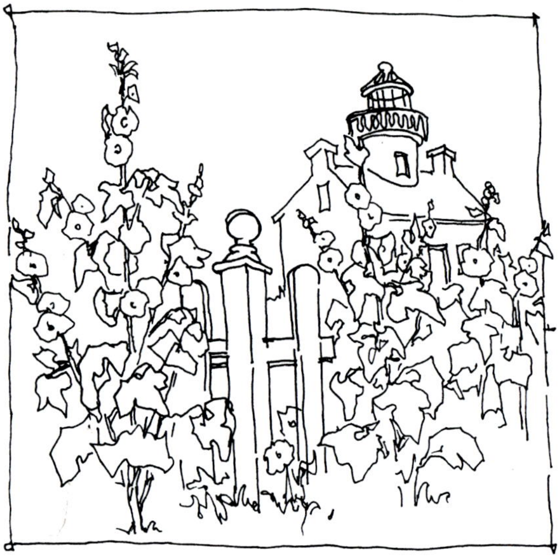

Square Format Three of the elements fit in a nice arrangement within the square, but the composition would be better if the building and fence post didn't meet right in the center of the scene. This is a common problem—and it happens to me more than I'd like to admit!

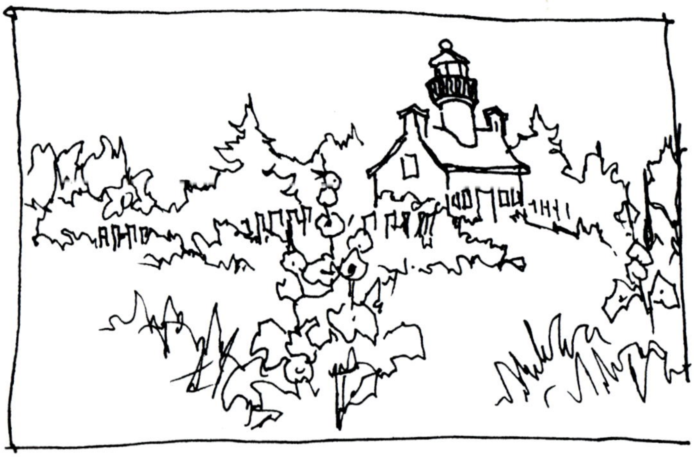

Landscape Format This is a nice arrangement. Not only do all five elements fit comfortably, but the building in the distance and the flowers in the foreground give this horizontal composition an open feeling and a good balance. The path is a great visual because it guides the viewer's gaze, moving it from the foreground to the point of interest (the lighthouse). I think I want to use this arrangement for my painting, but I'll still do a couple more format sketches before making a final decision.

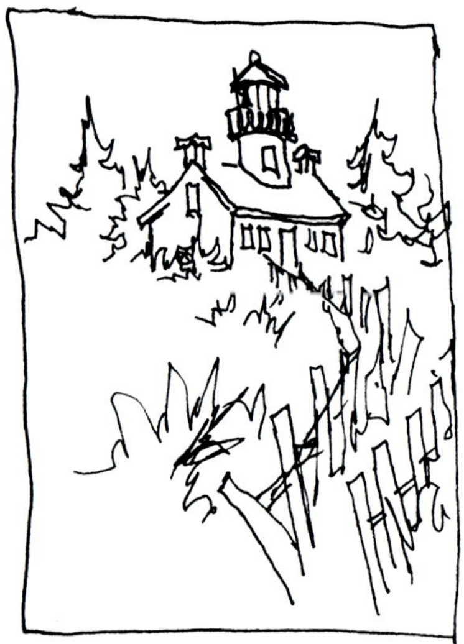

Portrait Format As with the landscape format, this vertical arrangement pushes the building into the background. But the fence in the lower right corner is drawing attention away from the center of interest.

Combining references and rearranging the elements allows you to bring your own personal perception to a photograph. If you're just copying a photo without involving your imagination, you may as well just frame the photo.

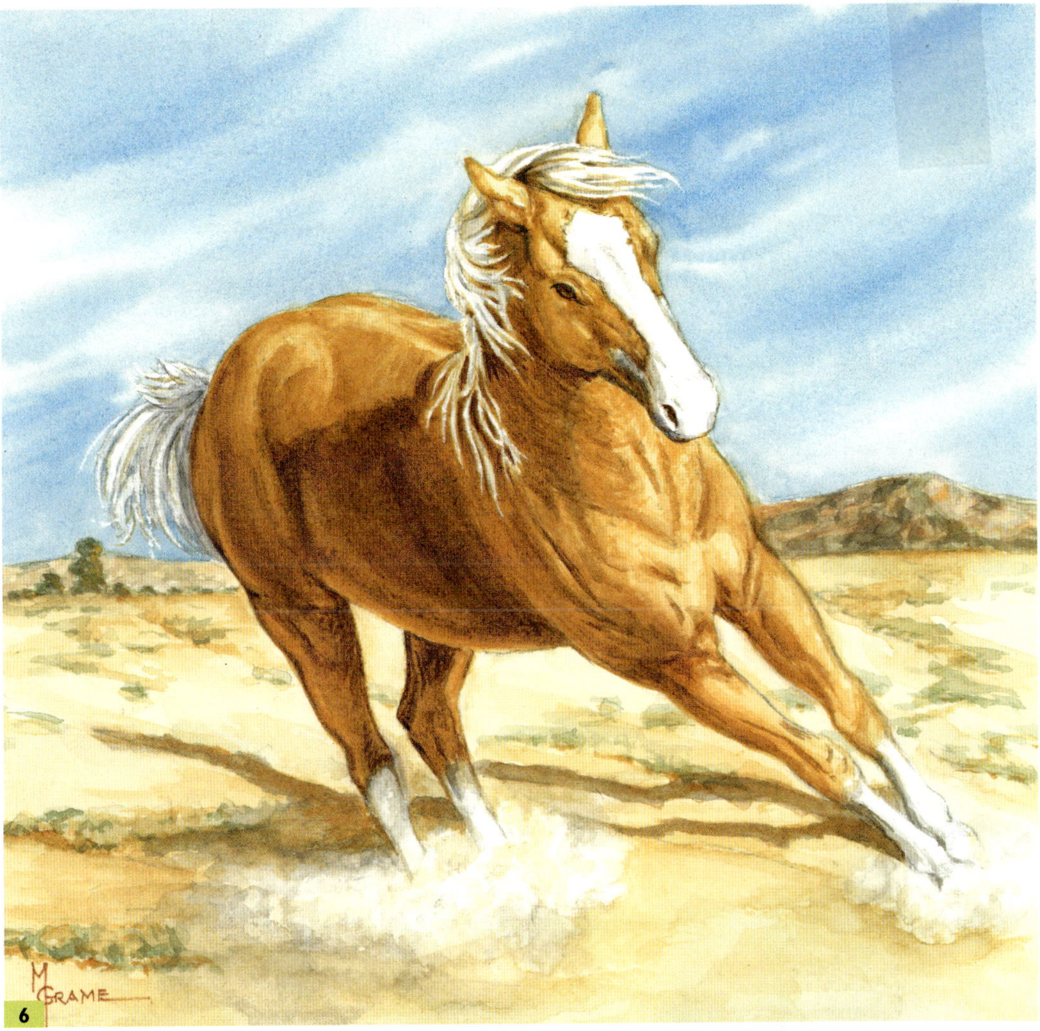

Step Six Now I add my darkest values. I glaze yellow ochre, raw sienna, and then burnt umber over the colt, letting each glaze dry before applying the next. Then I define the shadows in the whites and darken the cast shadows with a mix of Payne's gray and burnt sienna. I also continue refining the vegetation with the grayed sap green mix. I lightly wash over the dust cloud with the Payne's gray and burnt sienna mix and pat the damp area with a tissue. Finally I add highlights at the ends of the mane and tail by scraping off paint with a utility knife.

Lesson 7: Focusing on Reflections with Geri Medway

Water is an appealing subject because it can take so many different forms, from a peaceful still-water lake to a violent surging sea. And watercolor is a fluid medium that lends itself well to the subject of water and reflections. Keep in mind that the way water reflects its surroundings depends on whether the water is moving or is at rest. In moving water, reflections distort the size and shape of the objects being reflected, whereas in still water the reflections mirror the objects almost exactly. In this scene, Geri Medway illustrates how to paint the gentle movement of the harbor water and the slightly rippled reflections of the boats at dock.

Color Palette

cadmium red deep*, Indian yellow*, indigo blue*, peacock blue*, phthalo blue, ultramarine blue, white gouache

Water

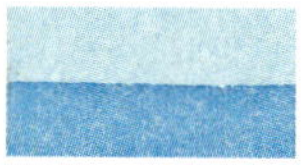

Phthalo blue (light and dark glazes)

Phthalo blue and a touch of ultramarine blue glaze

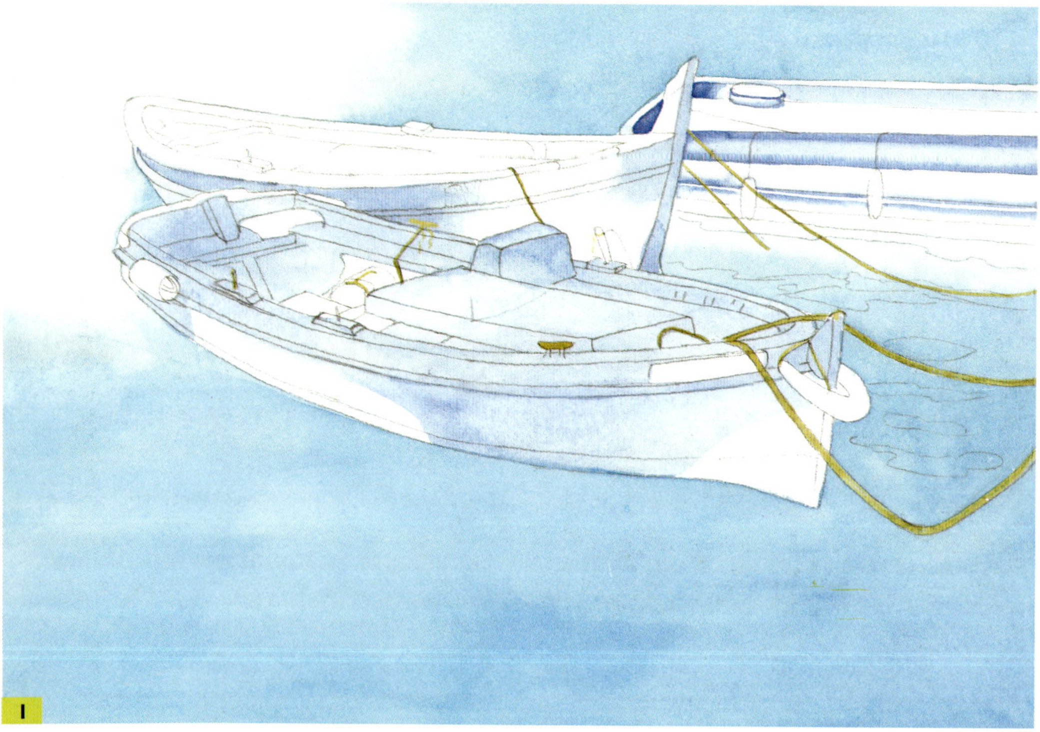

1

Step One Once my sketch is complete, I mask off the ropes with colored liquid frisket (see Masking Whites on page 42). When the frisket is dry, I start applying background washes with a large round brush. (I use one large round brush with a fine point throughout, and I use a separate brush for the clear water of my graded washes.) I begin by applying a thin ultramarine blue wash over the boats. When this is dry, I glaze a second, darker layer over the shadowed areas. Then I wash phthalo blue over the water area, taking care not to make the color too even. The slight inconsistencies in color will help create the illusion of movement in the water.

Painting from Life

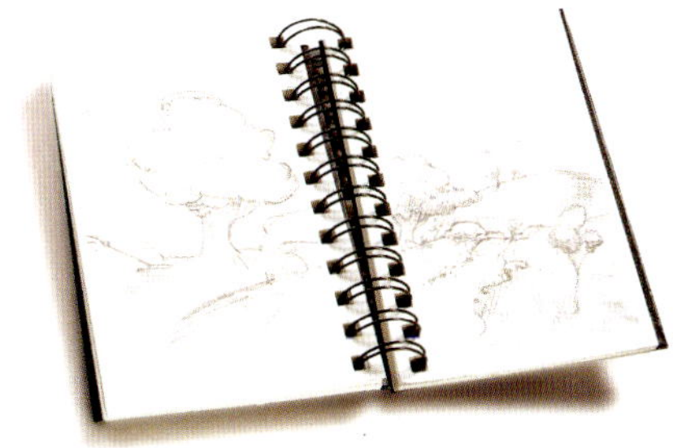

Photos are wonderful reference tools and are invaluable for many projects, such as depicting animals in motion or capturing a fleeting sunset. But nothing can quite compare to actually going out on location and experiencing your subject firsthand. Watercolor is an easily portable medium—most drawing boards have handles, the paints are available in transportable pans and small tubes, and the only additive you need is water. But you don't need to actually paint on location to reap the benefits of painting from life; you can learn just as much from detailed notes and drawings you make in a sketchbook. Take a small sketchbook wherever you go, and draw whatever attracts your eye. Make notes about colors, lighting, and the mood the scene evokes so you can re-create it later in your studio. Or just make quick, loose sketches of different subjects to help develop your artist's eye and practice your drawing skills. You'll find that your sketchbook will become a personal record book and a source of inspiration for future paintings.

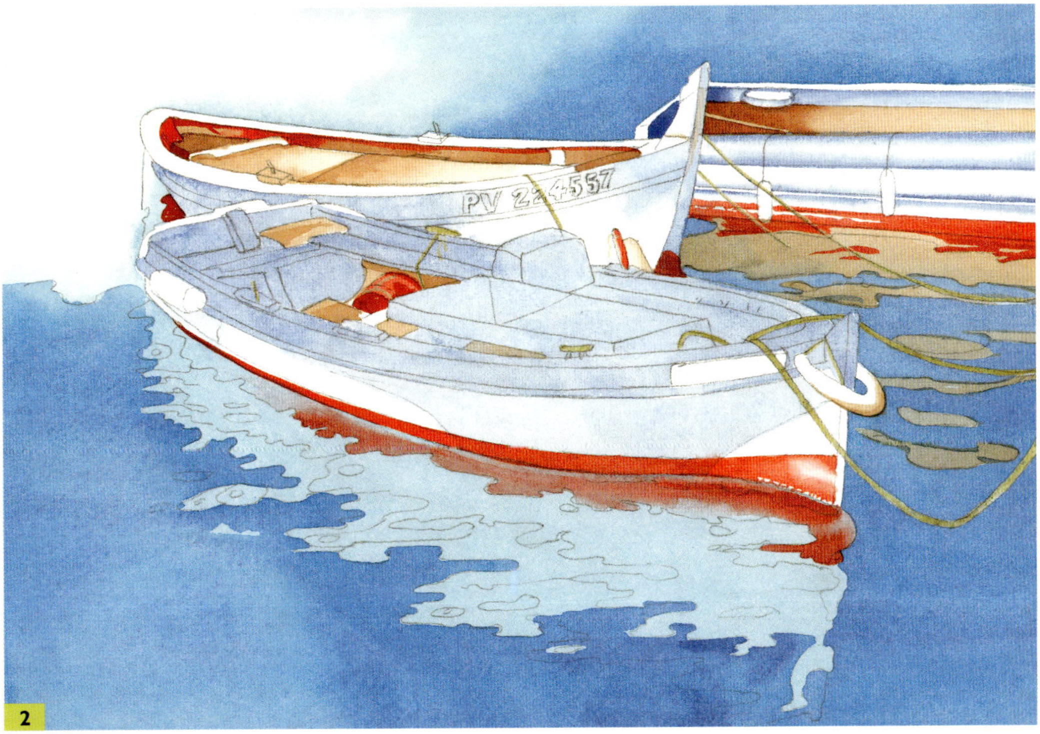

Step Two Now I start adding the colors, beginning with a thin glaze of burnt sienna for the brown areas. After the first layer has dried, I apply a second coat with a little more pigment and then repeat the process, building up successively darker layers. Then I add a flat wash of cadmium red deep to fill in the bottom edges around the boats, the buoys, and the reflections in the water. For the lighter values, I gradually add more water to each successive stroke. There is not much movement in the water, so the reflections are only slightly rippled. Next I lay in a second glaze of phthalo blue over the water, painting around the reflections. When dry, I add a little more depth with a third glaze using phthalo and a little ultramarine blue.

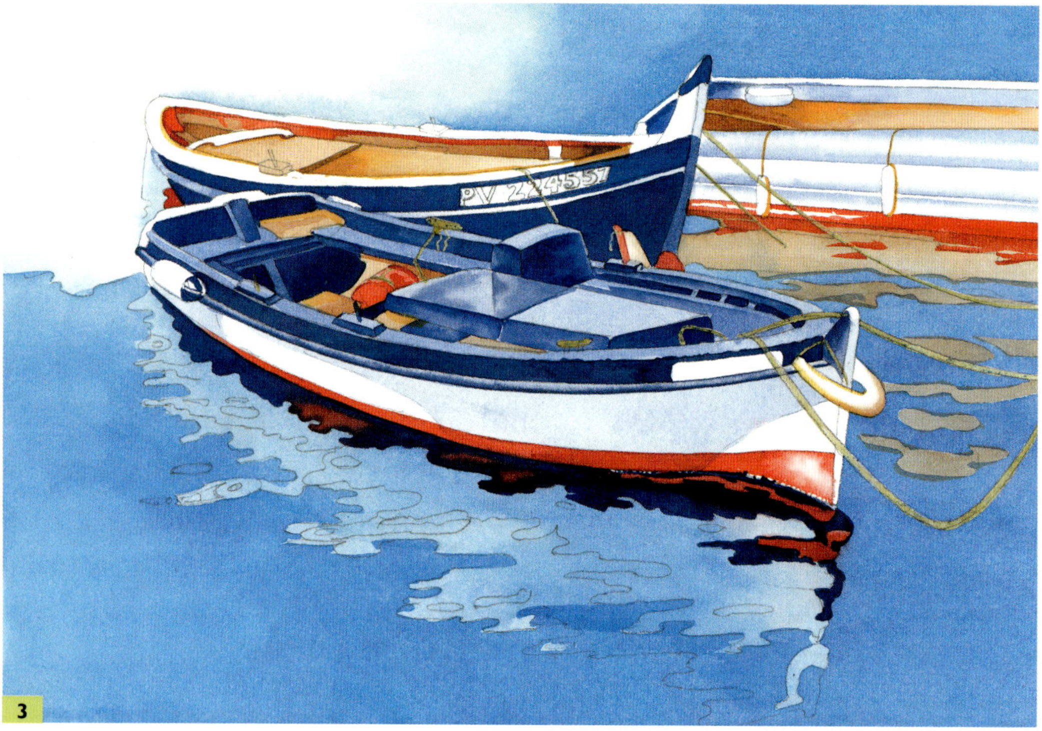

Step Three For the boat interiors, I begin with a thin layer of ultramarine blue. I let it dry and then apply a darker blue mix of indigo blue and ultramarine blue. (I use enough of the indigo blue to achieve a good, dark color but not so much that it overpowers the richness of the ultramarine blue.) Next I add touches of sunshine with a few strokes of Indian yellow along some of the inside edges of the boats.

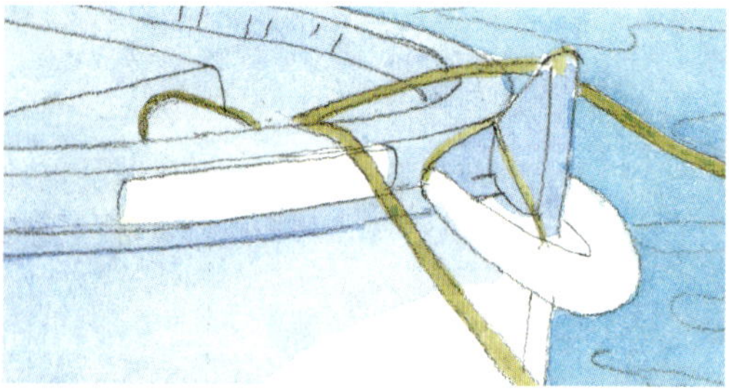

Masking Whites Detail To mask off the ropes (shown above) and other small white areas, I apply liquid frisket with a crow quill pen. The short, pointed nib of the pen allows me to work with careful precision inside the tight spaces and to achieve small, uniform lines.

Boat Interior

Indigo and ultramarine blue

Water Glaze

Peacock blue

Creating Ripples Detail To indicate the movement in the water, I brush clear water onto my surface. I don't wet it too thoroughly, as I want to maintain some control over how far my color spreads. Next I apply zigzagging strokes of peacock blue, letting the color bleed a little, as shown in the detail above.

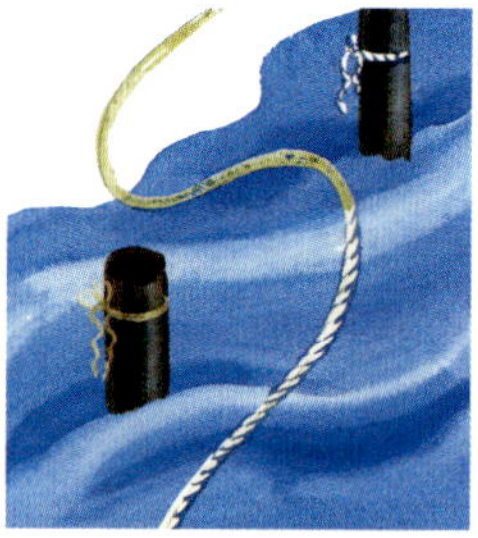

Finishing Detail When the painting is thoroughly dry, I gently rub away the dry frisket, revealing the white of the paper. Then I paint in the shadows and details with the pointed tip of a medium round brush and ultramarine blue. The example above shows the progression from applying the frisket to adding the details.

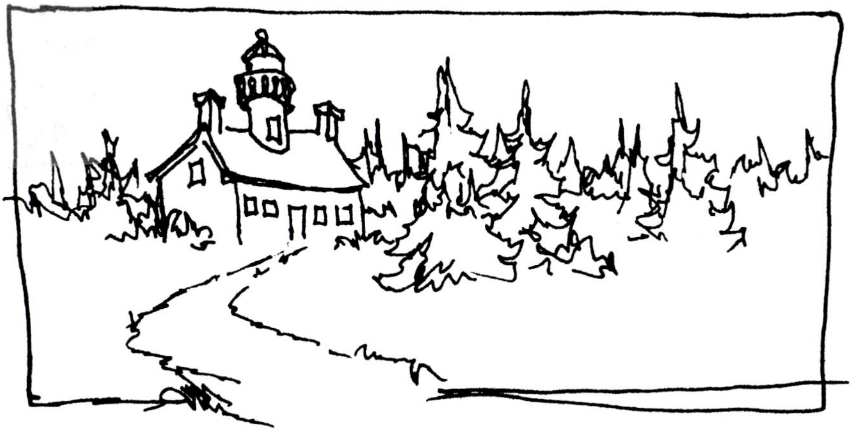

Panorama Format This wide horizontal format provides more space to work in, but it's difficult to fill with the elements on hand. There isn't enough going on to keep the viewer's attention.

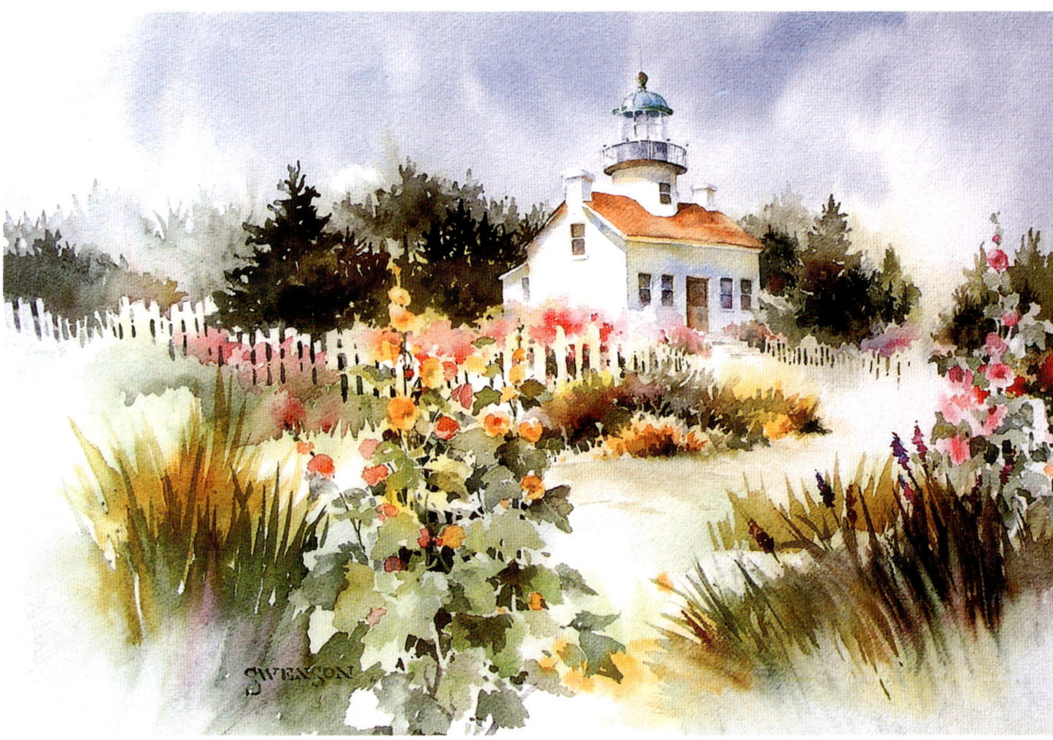

The landscape format that includes all five elements was the right choice for this finished piece. It would be impossible to create a painting with this much color or interest if you painted directly from the source without allowing your imagination its say!

True creativity takes what you know and makes it more than it was.

Step Two: Determine the Values

Values (or light and dark variations) say more than color. You can use the most glorious colors in the world, but superior values will triumph over color every time! The capacity to evaluate and apply correct values is one of the most important skills an artist can learn. If the drawing is the skeleton of a painting, then the values are the muscular structure that holds the body together and provides its form. When you create a value study, you create a solid structural plan for your painting.

The Value Scale

A value scale presents the range of lights to darks that a subject might comprise. The values on the scale shown below range from 1 to 10, with 10 being the darkest value. An object in bright light with a cast shadow might have values running from 1 (an area in direct light) to 10 (parts of the shadows). But not all subjects will contain a full range of values like the one shown here. For example, a misty, cold scene might have values that would linger on the lower end of the scale, ranging from 2 to 6. You can create a strong value study with as few as five separate values.

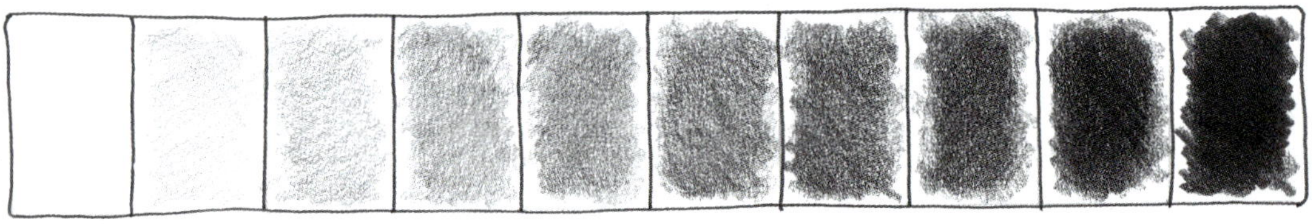

The Value Study

Much like Step One, Step Two is about using your imagination. When you make a value study, you're taking what you see (the actual values of your subject) and interpreting them, altering them in such a way that makes your painting stronger. Value studies allow you to explore the possibilities before you begin painting.

Always make multiple value studies of a subject before you paint it so you can view your many options. Working with small format thumbnails (2" x 4" or 3" x 5") makes this task more approachable.

Perceiving Values Before you can adjust the values of your subject, you must first be able to recognize the original values. Color has a way of misleading the eye when you're trying to distinguish values in a photo. You can photocopy your reference in black and white (or print a black-and-white copy from your computer) to help. Or you can skip the technology and just do as the Masters did: Squint!

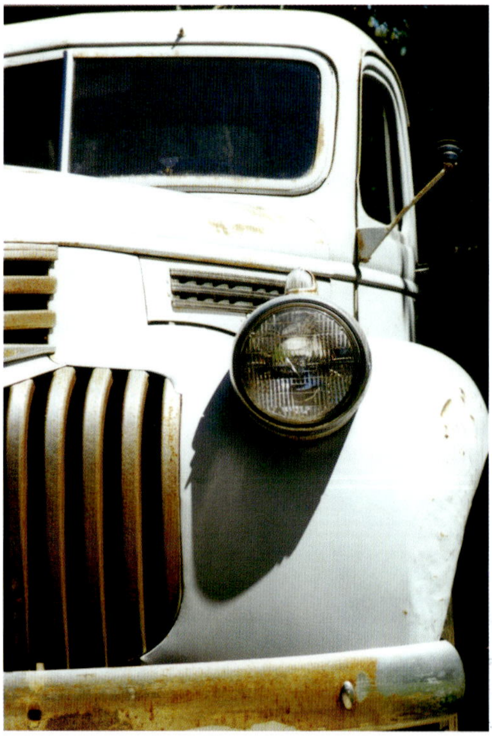

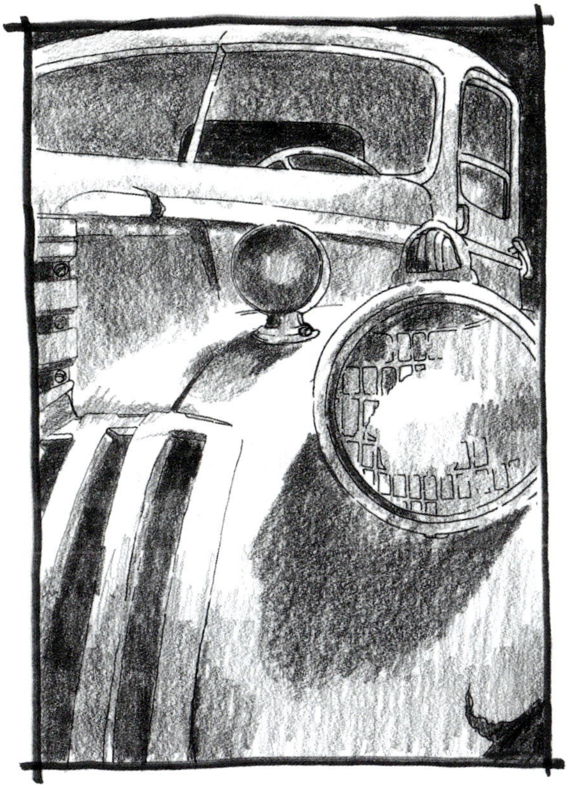

Value Study 1 Although this value study is a nice drawing, there isn't anything very exciting going on with the value placement. The values are all too similar, making for a boring composition. Pumping up the contrasts might make all the difference.

Color gets all the glory, but value does all the work!

If redrawing the image to make several value studies puts you off, make a few black-and-white photocopies of your initial sketch and work out your studies on them. You can still try out multiple ideas without feeling hindered by the repetition.

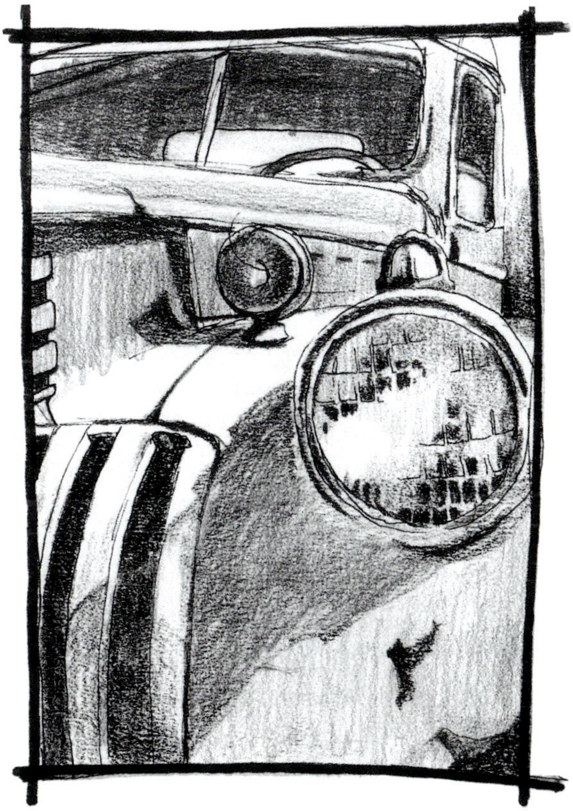

Value Study 2 The second drawing is better—but there is one big problem: The longer shadow from the headlight draws attention away from the focal point (the headlight), and it's leading the eye into the lower left-hand corner, someplace it shouldn't go.

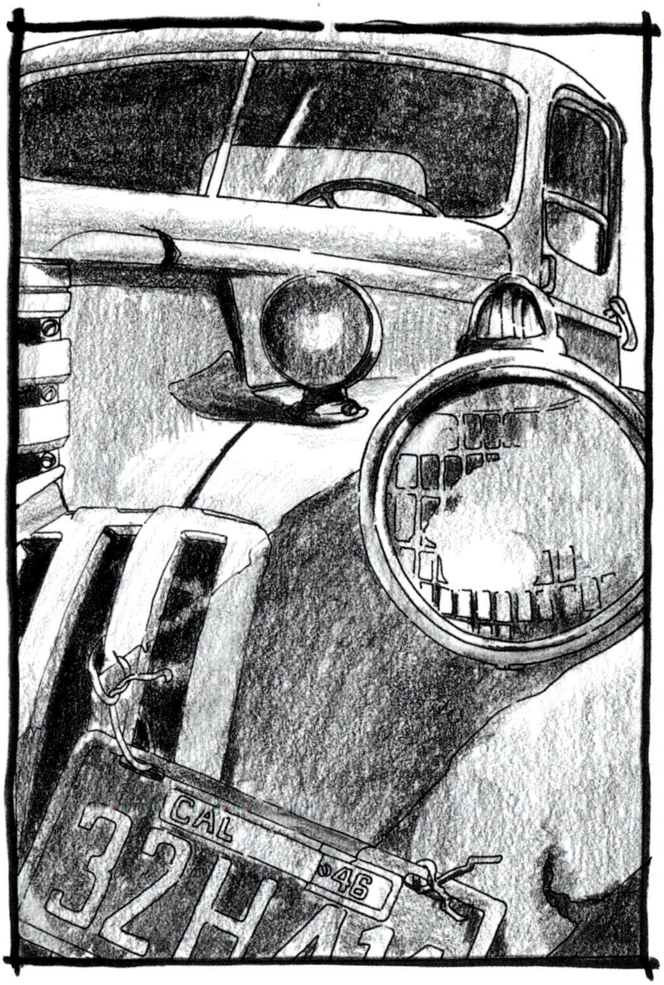

Value Study 3 Build upon your previous accomplishments as you make each new value study. This revision mimics the second study, but with one vital change: the addition of a license plate. The plate provides the shape and value needed to redirect the eye back up into the focal area. If you need to make more than three value studies, do so. Keep trying, making small adjustments until you get it right. Remember, now is the time to make any necessary changes, not after you start painting.

Strengthening the Composition with Value Placement

When working out your value study, your goal is to enhance the composition by creating interest and giving the eye a clear path to follow. Altering the original values of my reference allows me to create a strong composition that leads the eye through the scene. This composition design is suggested by the original reference, but the value placements enhance the S shape—which runs through the dark values in the shadow on the fender, through the lighter-valued headlamp, and up into the dark values of the windows at top.

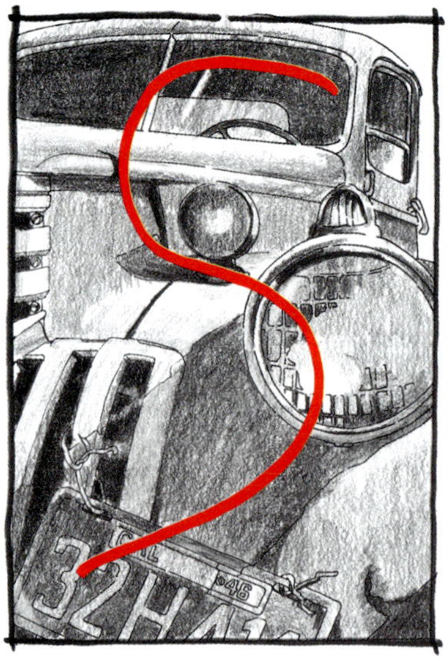

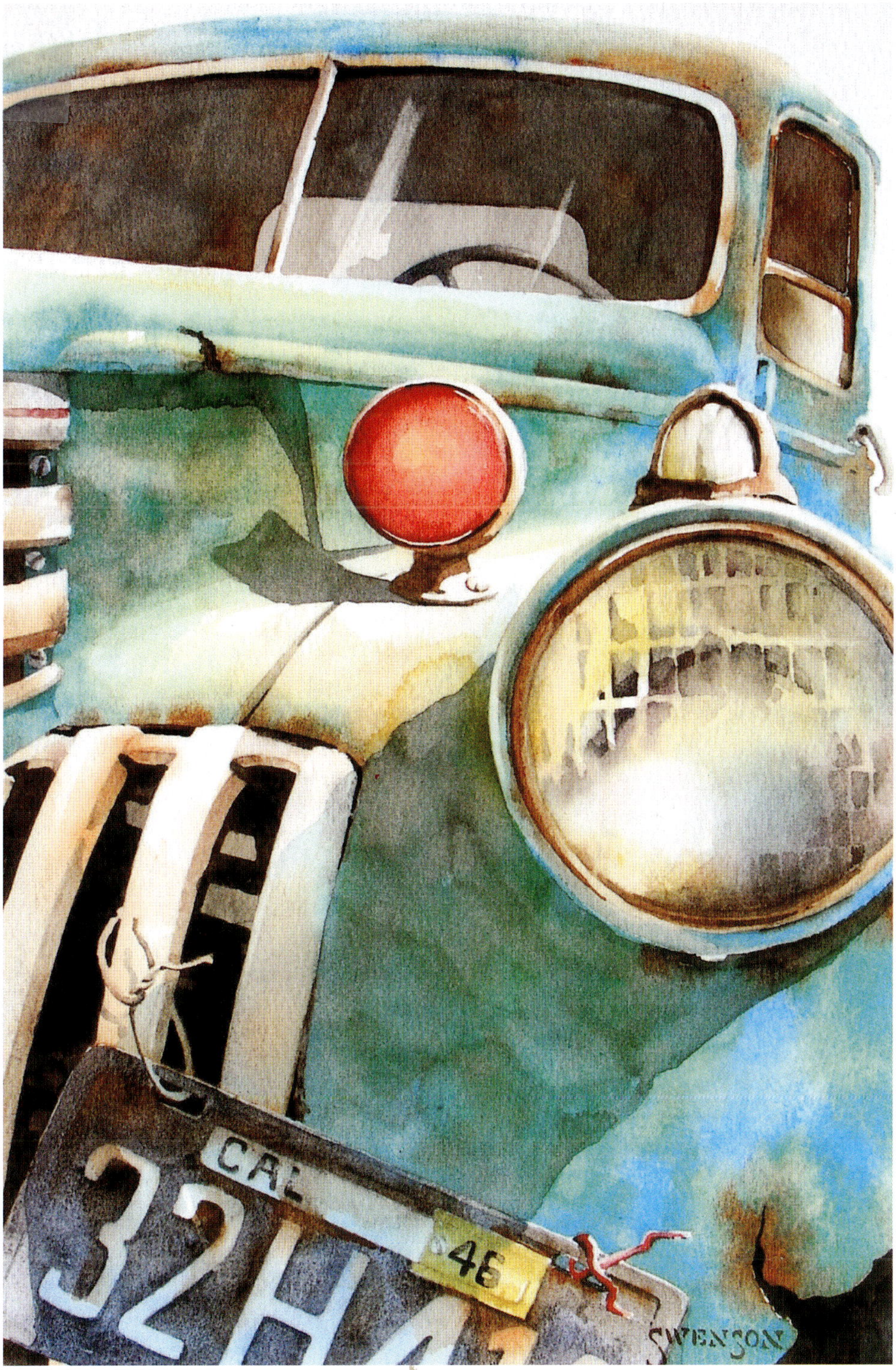

Notice how much more "pop" the final painting has in comparison with the original reference? That is a result of the value study. The deeper colors are representative of the darker values that were chosen to make a stronger painting. If you squint your eyes, you should see a near replica of the third value study!

Step Three: Be Aware of Color

What originally attracted me to watercolor was the jewel-like quality of the medium—the way the colors seemed to dance on the surface of the paper. I chose the colors on my palette after many years of experience, through trial and error. My reasons for liking a color may not be yours; to use color effectively, you'll need to become aware of your options and experiment to find what colors work best for you. The colors you choose will become part of your language as an artist, and discovering the potential in color will help you develop your own voice as an artist.

Paint Characteristics

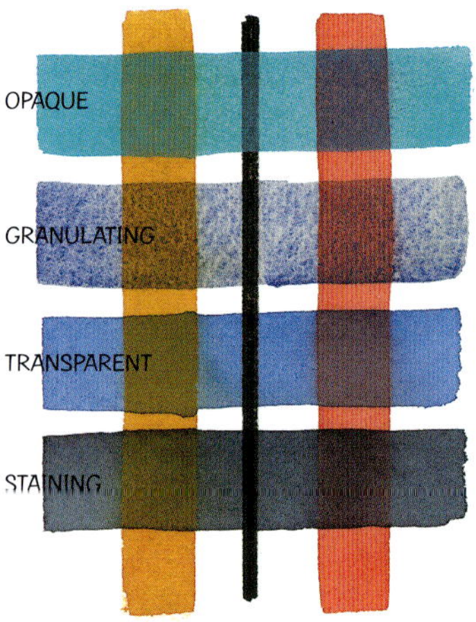

FOUR BLUE PAINTS—PAINTED OVER YELLOW AND RED TO TEST TRANSPARENCY.

Pigment Traits Pigments fall into four general categories: transparent, opaque, staining, and granulating. Transparent pigments are so finely textured that they can appear as clear as tinted glass. Opaque paints have a chalky appearance when dry. Staining colors are synthetic, dye-based pigments that can't be completely lifted out; they can easily overpower a painting if not used with care. Granulating colors are heavy and have a coarser grind.

TEST FOR STAINING AND LIFTABILITY

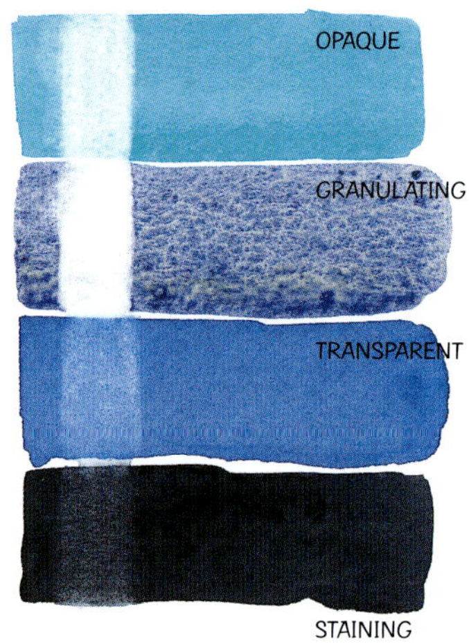

Keeping Records

To help keep track of different colors' qualities, take notes about all the paints you try. In addition to keeping a binder full of color swatches that I've created to test the characteristics of individual colors, I also have sketchbooks full of color-mixing exercises, providing a record of how different colors interact and relate to one another.

CUPRIC GREEN DEEP

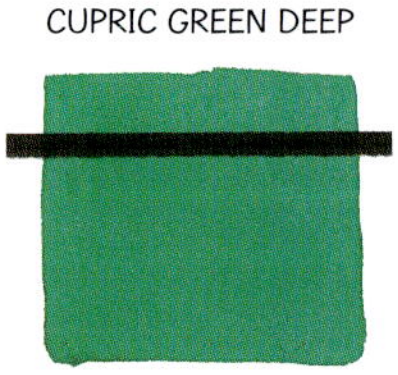

LEMON YELLOW

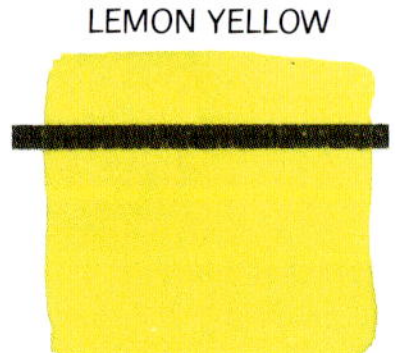

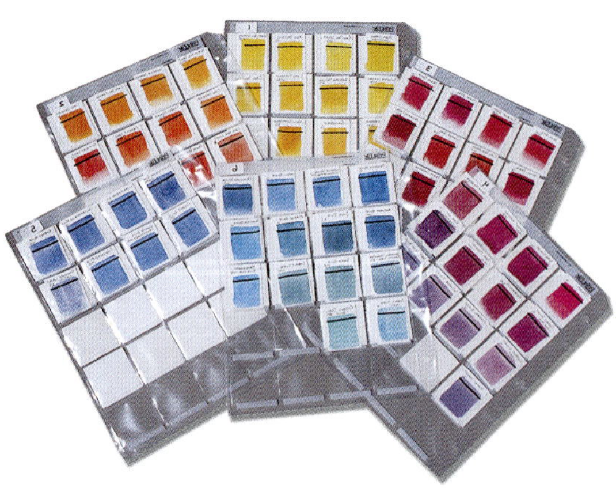

Color Swatches Make a color swatch with a transparency test (see page 11). Then record the paint's name and manufacturer.

▶ Color Mixing One of the best ways to learn about color is to play with it! Without any specific purpose, start mixing and matching colors. As you play, you'll find bad combinations as well as unexpectedly good ones!

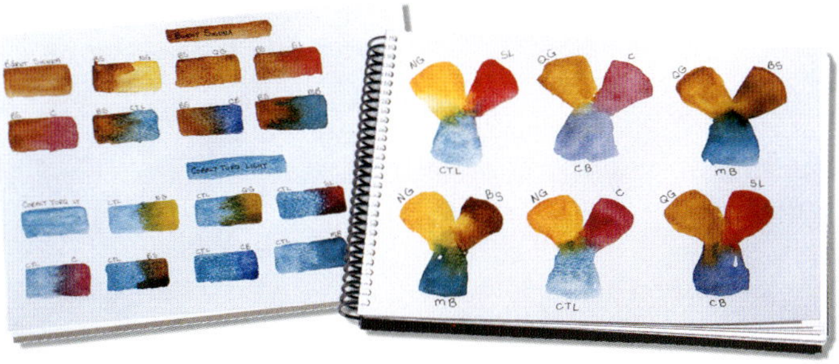

Color and Emotion

When deciding which colors to use, think about what you are trying to convey in your painting or what emotion you want to associate with the scene. If you want a tranquil scene, you should use colors that are calm and quiet—cool colors. But if you want a joyful and lively painting, you should incorporate colors that are bright and happy—warm colors. (See page 26 for more about color temperature.) Your color choices affect how the painting is received by the viewer and what emotion they attach to it.

CALM

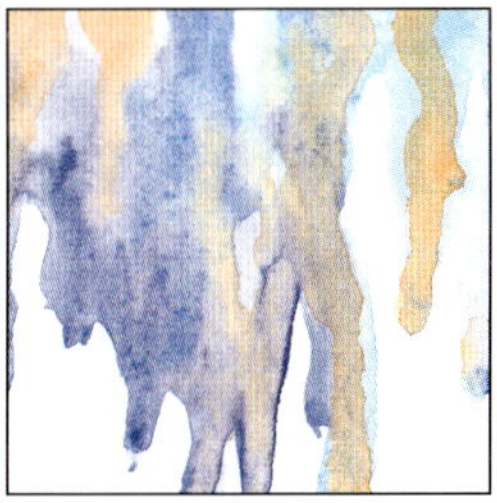

SAD

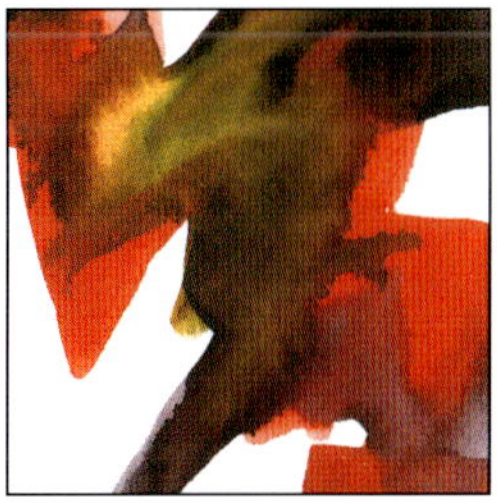

ANGRY

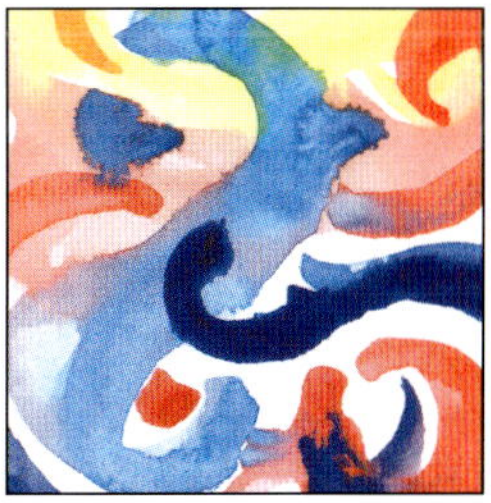

HAPPY

Each of these examples clearly displays an emotion. Think about how the color influences your perception of each one. Of course, it takes more than color to state emotion—but it's a strong start!

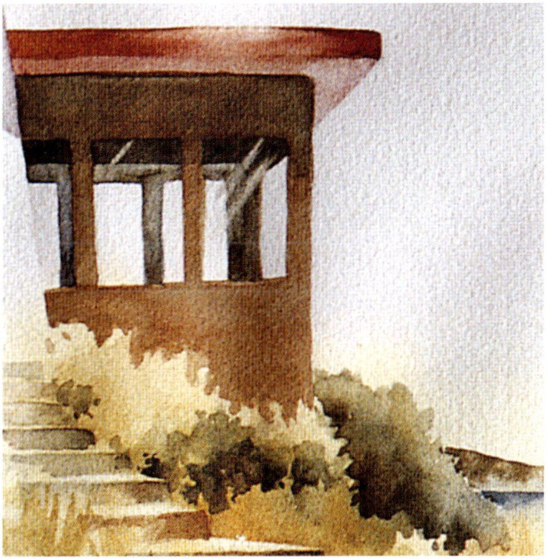

Clear Skies The same subject can take on a very different feeling depending on color choice. In this scene, the sun is out, and warm colors help convey an overall mood that is upbeat and cheerful.

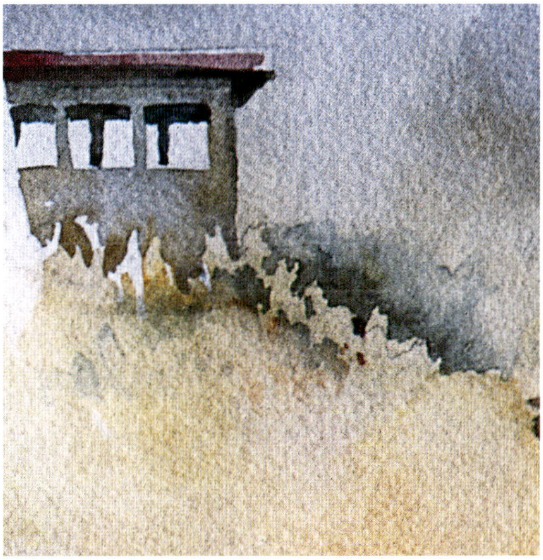

Stormy Weather Here is a similar scene right after a storm. The sky is gray and moody, and the cool, muted colors help express a quiet, more sedate mood.

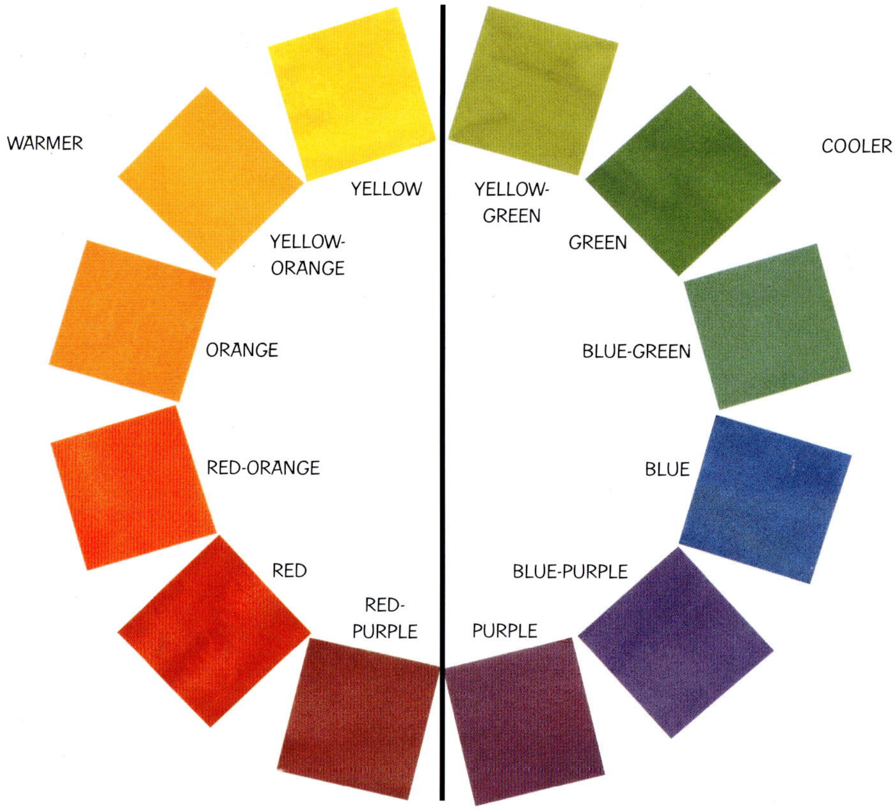

Color Temperature Colors on the "warm" side of the color wheel (yellows, oranges, and reds) are full of life and vitality. Colors on the "cool" side (greens, blues, and purples) evoke a sense of calm and tranquility. But every color has both warm and cool hues too. For example, scarlet lake is a warm red hue and permanent carmine is a cool red hue. Keeping a warm and a cool version of each color on your palette provides a lot of versatility.

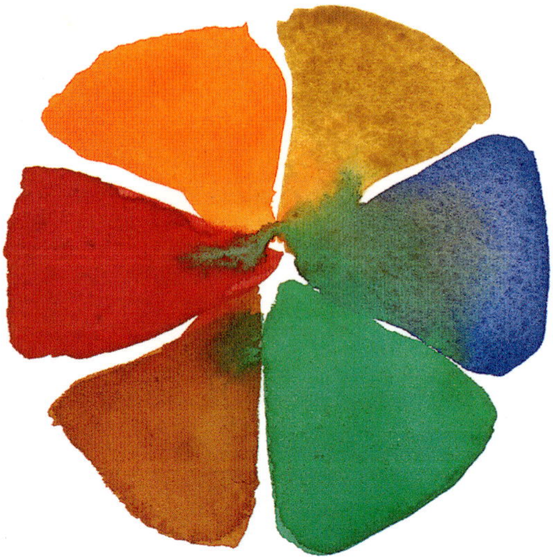

◀ **Combining Tones** Working with predominantly cool tones doesn't prohibit the use of warm colors. This subject's palette contains cools and warms: raw sienna, ultramarine light, cupric green deep, burnt sienna, permanent carmine, and permanent orange.

▲ **Neutralizing Colors** Pure color can be commanding, but strong color everywhere can be distracting. Mix a color with a little of its complement to tone it down without making it dull or flat.

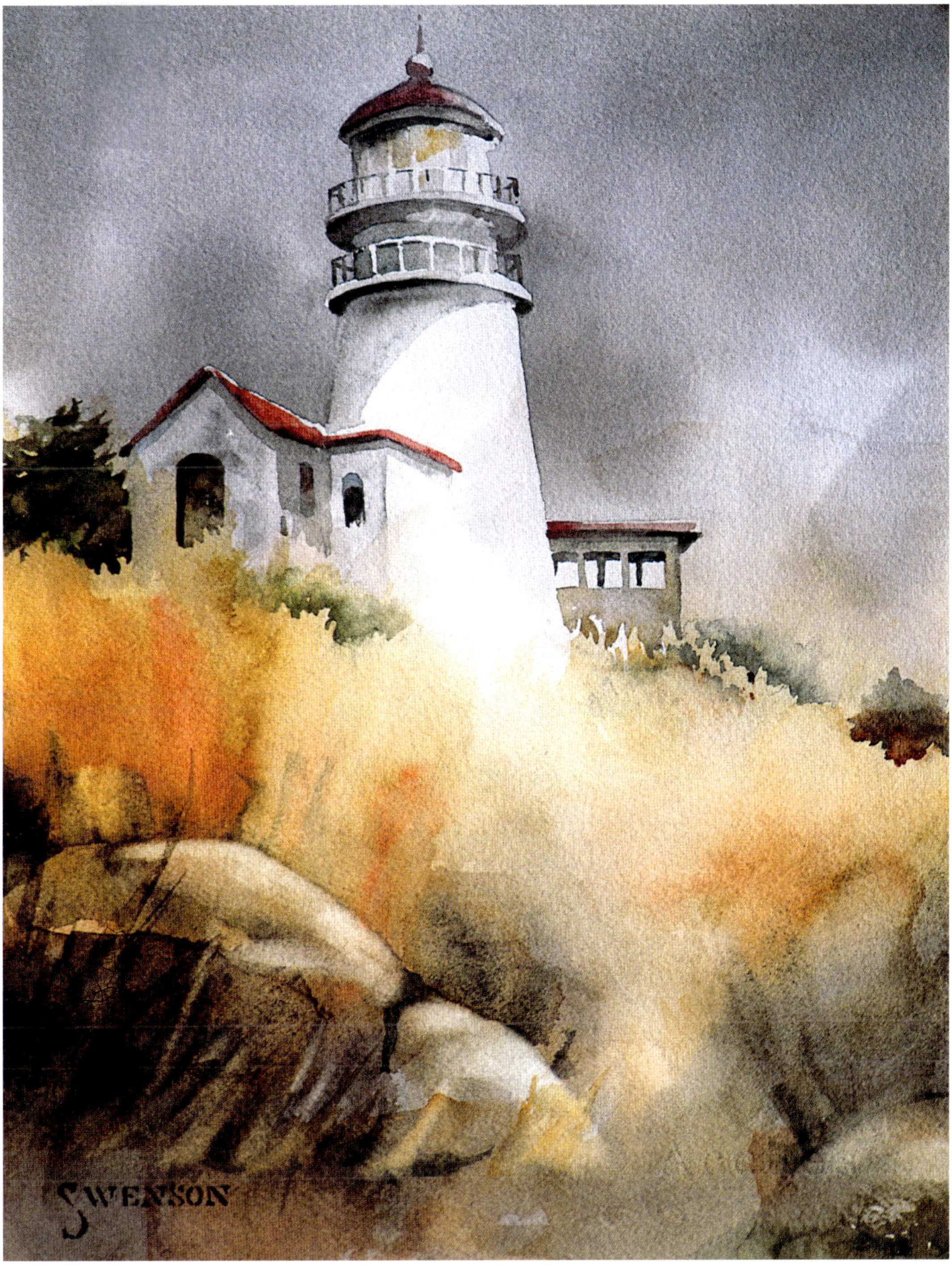

This painting has a cool dominance because of the gray used in the sky and foreground—the mix of permanent carmine and cupric green deep has a slight separation of color that adds energy and interest to the large areas. The yellow-orange foliage provides just the right accent against the gray tones, and an application of the same yellow-orange in the lighthouse window balances the warm colors in the lower section of painting—a technique called "echoing color."

Step Four: Develop a Center of Interest

The center of interest in a painting is similar to the lead character in a play. If there were no lead, how would you know whose story to follow? A good artist consciously chooses to make one area of a composition more important and dominant than the rest. It's okay to create other areas of interest—after all, a main character needs a supporting cast—but make sure the center of interest is evident to your audience.

To effectively develop a center of interest, you must do two things effectively: place the focal point and direct the viewer's eye to it. To do so, you'll not only want to manipulate the composition of your painting, you'll also want to consider the colors, values, sizes, and details of the many objects within it.

Placing the Center of Interest

Where should the center of interest be located? As a general rule, it's best to avoid corners, the center of the composition, or areas that are too high or too low. Many artists divide the picture plane into thirds to form a grid, which is used as a guide to place the elements of the composition. Called the "rule of thirds" or the "intersection of thirds," this principle involves dividing your picture plane into thirds, both vertically and horizontally. The rule of thirds is reliable, it's easy to follow, and it works for nearly all subject matter and every type of format.

▶ **Direct the Eye with Angles** Arrange the elements so the center of interest is located at an intersection point. Use the other aspects of the composition to support the focal point. Angled lines like sloping roofs and fences act as natural arrows, pointing the eye toward the center of interest!

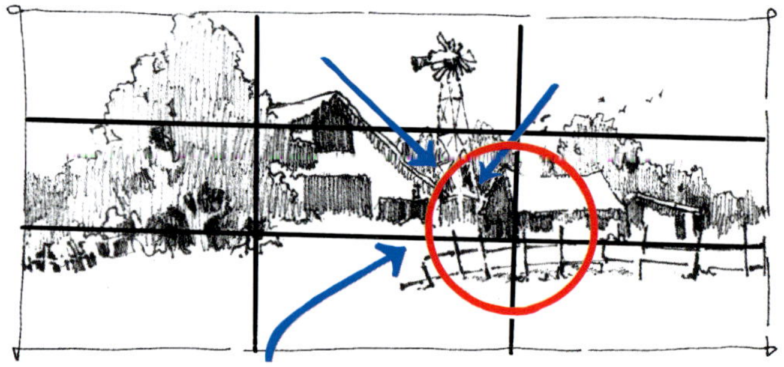

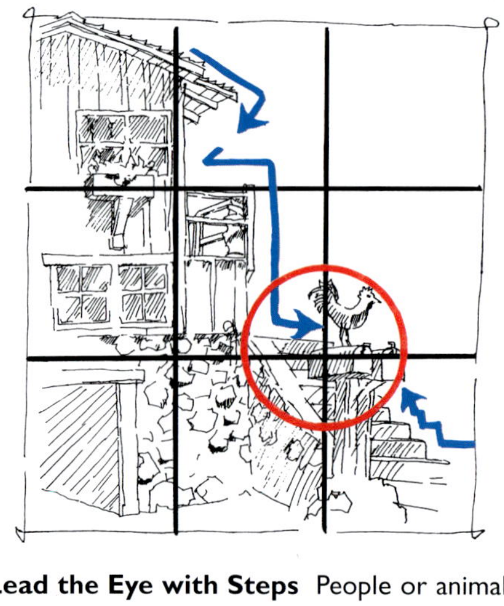

Lead the Eye with Steps People or animals instantly grab attention, so they make ideal centers of interest. And stairs or steplike paths are ideal ways to lead the eye directly to a point of interest!

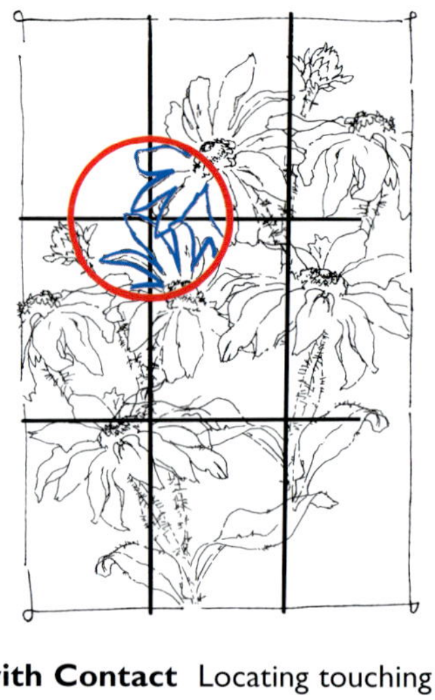

Lead with Contact Locating touching or connecting items at an intersection point will build interest by creating tension. Value and color would help delineate this center of interest even more.

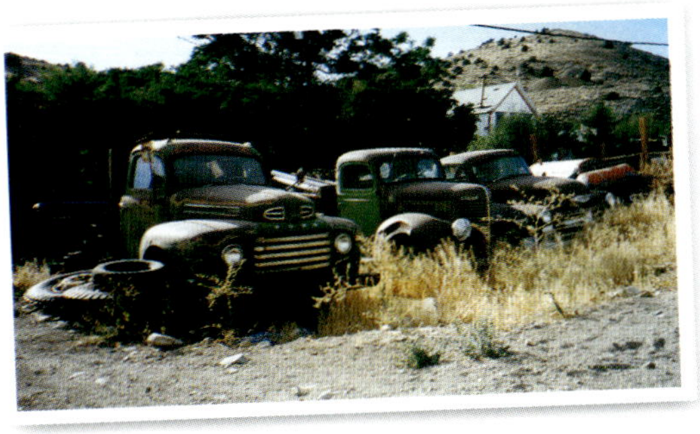

◀ **Photo References** It's rare that a photo reference will have a strong, naturally established focal point. In this landscape-format photo, the trucks are centered between the top and bottom, and there is too much space on the left side. Not exactly a favorable composition!

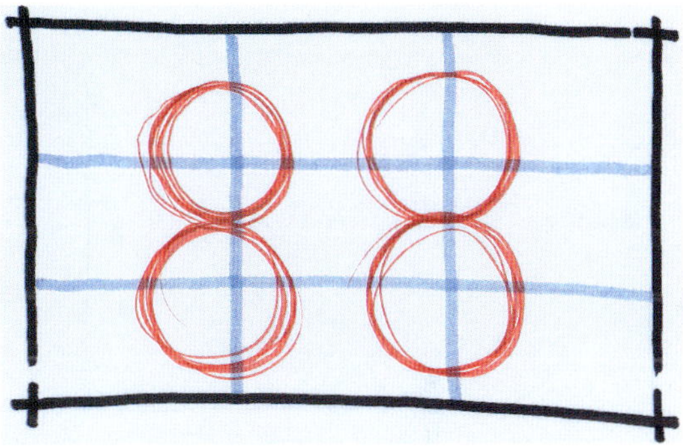

▶ **Drawing the Grid** As you gain experience, you'll be able to visualize the intersection of thirds as it applies to your composition without drawing lines. But for now, work out a thumbnail as it applies to the proportions of your painting. Using the basic rules of thirds as your guide, you'll have four choices for placing your center of interest.

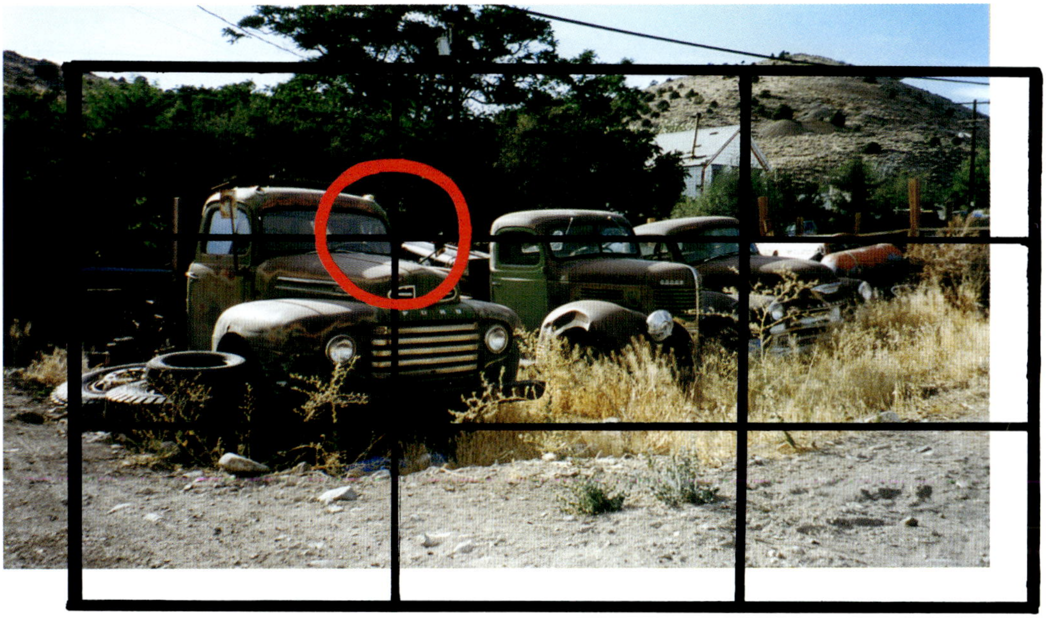

Deciding Placement With a little luck, a clear choice will present itself, as it has here. The top left intersection was a good match for the main truck. If a clear answer doesn't present itself, you should consider rearranging the elements of your painting (see pages 16–17).

Unlike the camera, which focuses on everything at once, the human eye and brain are discerning and can focus only on the thing that is of interest.

Directing the Viewer's Eye

Once you've decided on a good location for the center of interest, how are you going to guide the viewer's eye to it? There are various methods for capturing a viewer's attention and directing it around a painting, including the effective use of color, activity, value, size, detail, and sharpness.

Directing with Color

Placing complementary colors next to each other is an instant attention grabber. Set your center of interest against its complementary color to make it stand out immediately—and avoid pairing the supporting elements with their complements so they don't fight for attention. You don't need very much of a complement to draw the eye; if a complement is overused, it will become distracting.

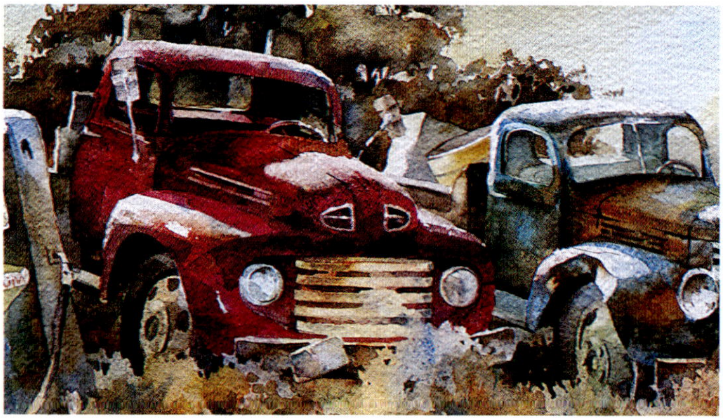

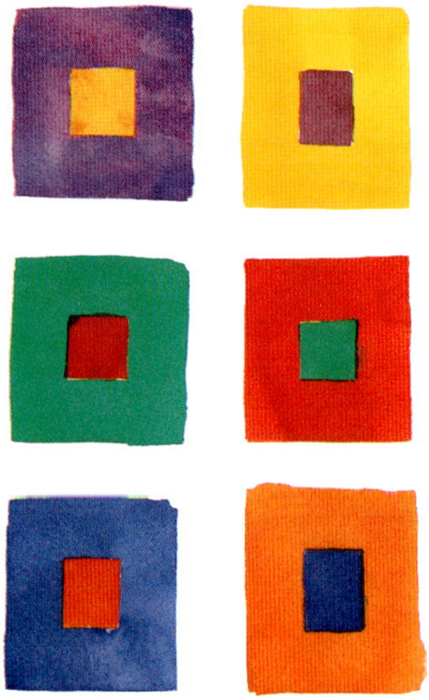

Red Against Green In the reference photo, both the foliage and main truck are green. But a red truck will have more contrast against the greenery. The most vivid and striking color pairings are always complements, such as those shown at right.

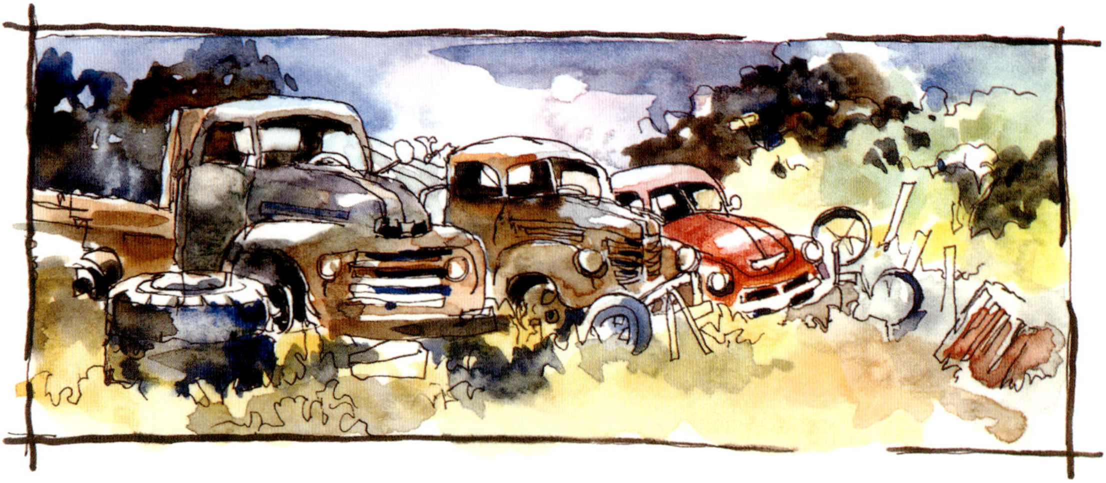

Using Red A complementary pairing isn't the only reason red makes a good choice for the main truck. Red attracts attention (as any matador will tell you!). For this reason, be careful when using red outside the focal area—here your eye is drawn away from the center of interest.

Directing with Activity

Another way to draw attention to a specific area is to include activity. Adding dense foliage, overlapping objects, and eye-catching elements such as people or signs are all ways to introduce activity into the focal area. As with the grouped mass composition, the center of interest should be where objects are most densely situated and where the most overlap occurs. It's important to balance all that activity with areas of calm—so as you move away from the focal area, use less contrast and detail.

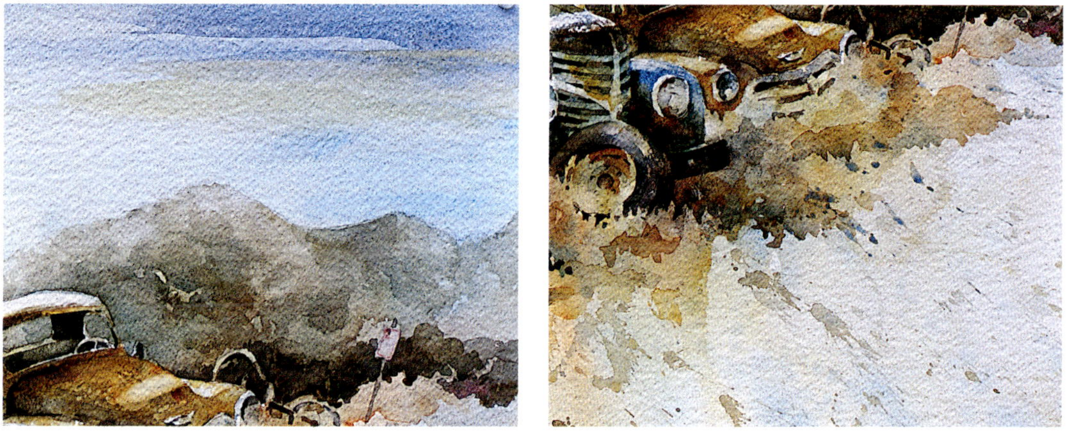

Calm Areas If all parts of a painting are filled with activity, the eye has no place to rest. Keep the busyness centered around your focal point, and create neighboring areas of calm, like the open sky and unobtrusive foreground shown here. Calm areas may appear boring or dull when viewed on their own, but they're important for balance.

Signage

There is something about the printed word that immediately captures our attention. Have you ever looked at a sign without reading it? For this reason, adding signage near a center of interest can guide the viewer's eye in that direction.

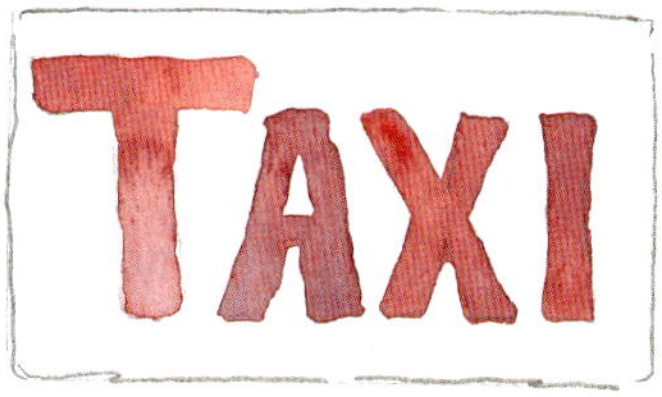

Detailed If lettering is too bold, crisp, or straightforward, it will draw too much interest.

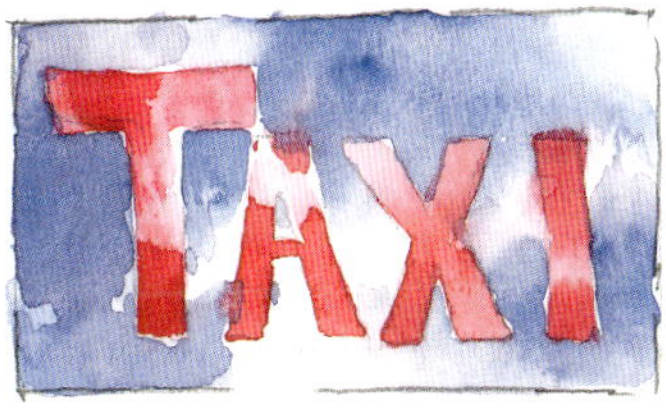

Subtle Subtlety is key when it comes to signs. This rendition is a better approach; it doesn't look as much like an advertisement for a product.

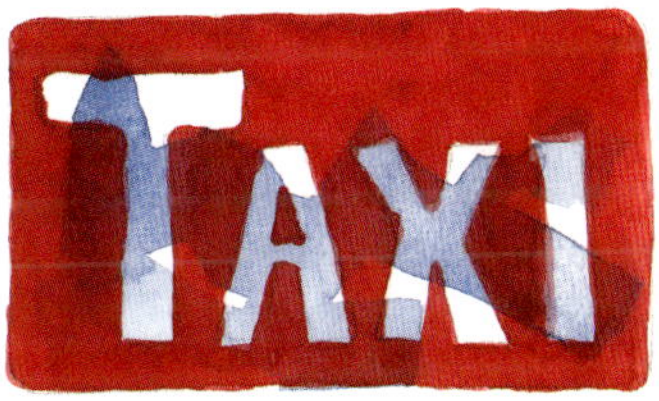

Suggestion To keep signage from becoming too dominant, consider toning down the words by glazing over them with another color.

Directing with Value

Creating contrast with lights and darks in a focal area is like painting a bull's-eye on the center of interest! Take the time to carefully determine where to place values by making a study before you paint. Strategic placement of values is actually more important than the color itself. Save the extremes of both light and dark values for your focal point; the rest of the composition should be kept more moderate.

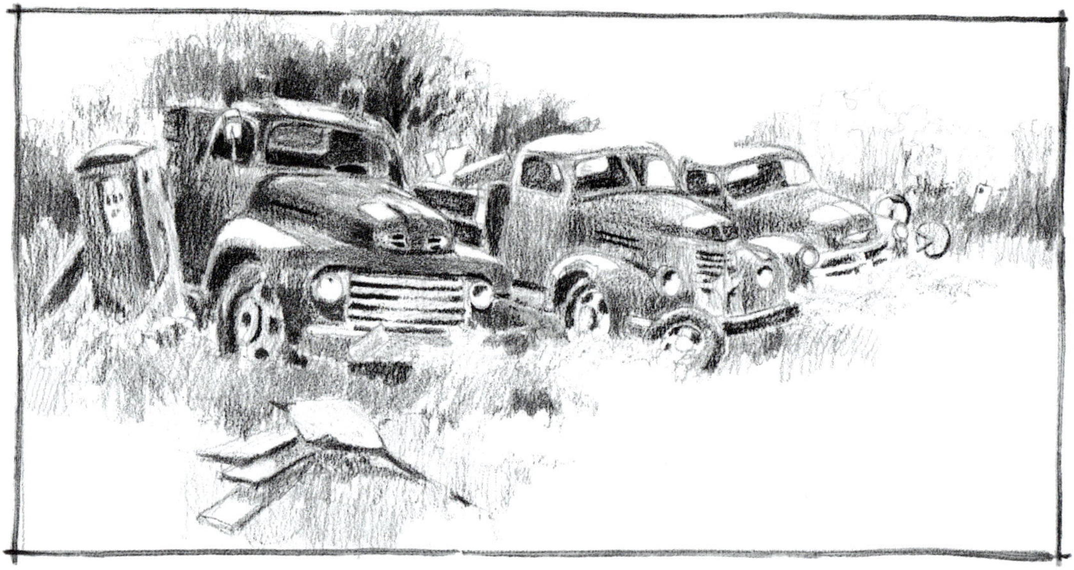

Drawing Attention To accentuate the focal point in this scene, I place the darkest values inside the cab of the dominant truck, contrasting those values with the light, nearly white values on the top of the cab and on the hood.

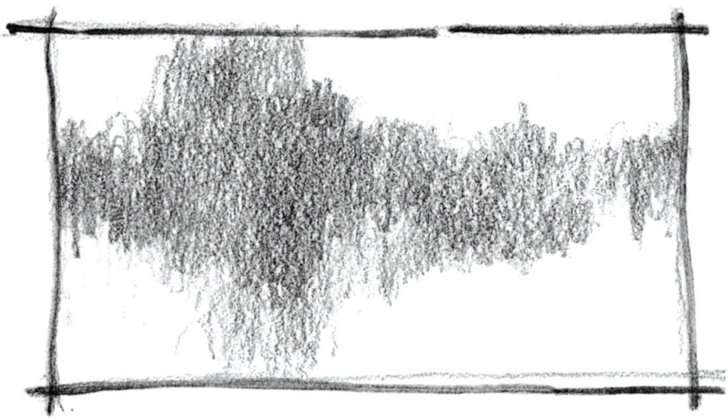

Cruciform Values The placement of the values also emphasizes the structural shape of the composition. Notice that the deepest values are concentrated in the center of the cruciform, balanced by the light values in each of the four corners.

> *"Learn diligence before speedy execution."*
> *—Leonardo da Vinci*

Directing with Size, Detail, and Sharpness

At this point, it should go without saying that the main subject matter (the very reason you are creating the painting) should be dominant in size when compared with the other elements in the painting. But you may not know that it should also have the greatest amount of detail and sharpness.

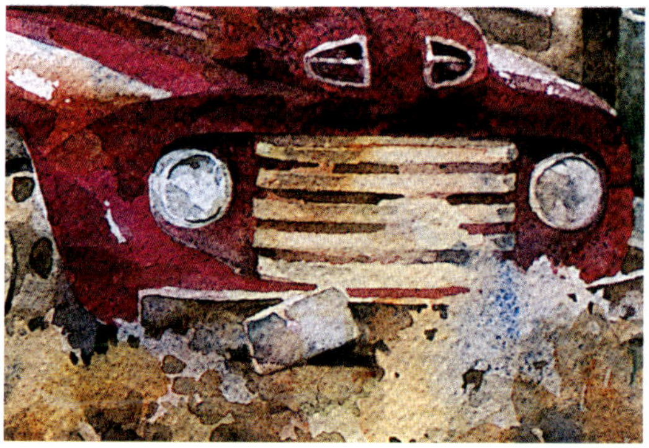

Focusing In The large truck in the foreground has the greatest amount of detail and the most definite edges.

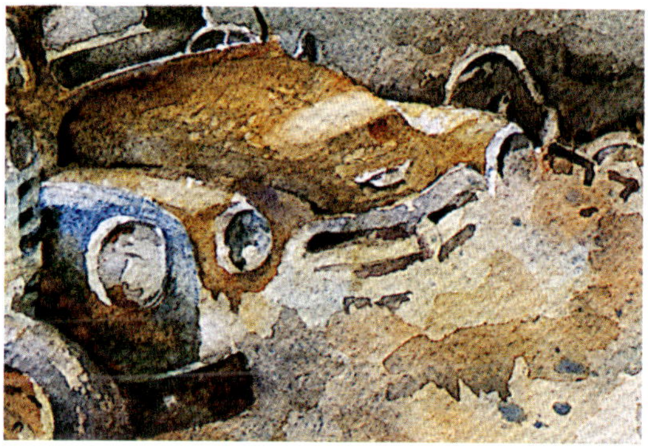

Blurring Out In contrast, the truck in the distance has much less detail. Many of its edges are incomplete or become lost and disappear into the weeds.

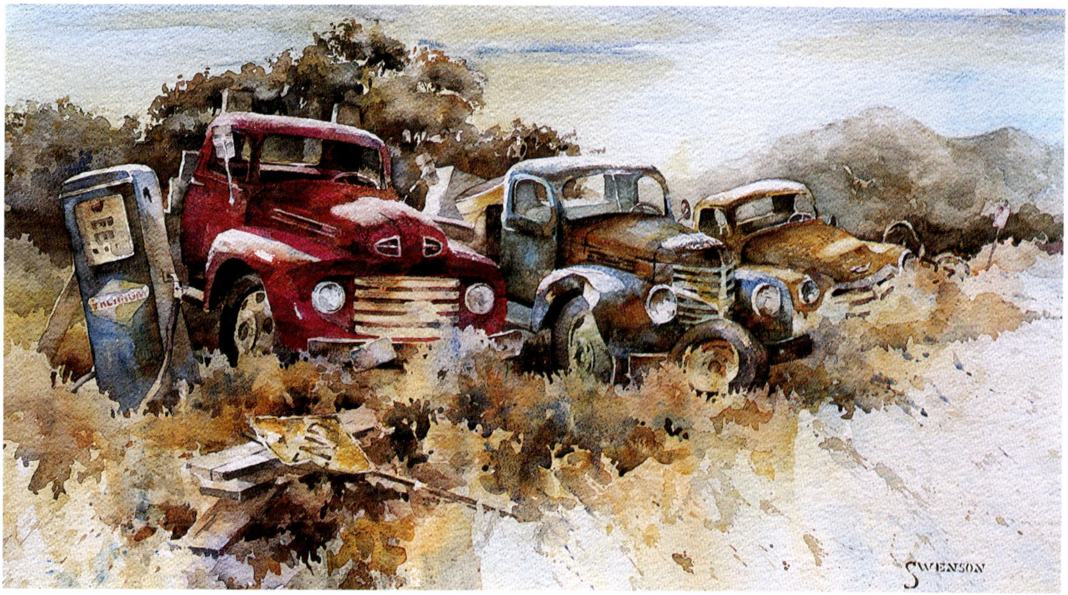

All your planning becomes worthwhile when you see the finished product. There is no question about where the eye should go in this painting—it automatically rests on the red truck, where color, value, activity, size, detail, sharpness, and even signage have directed it!

Step Five: Form a Visual Passage

It's wonderful to know that you can guide the viewer's eye wherever you want it to go! Although establishing a center of interest is a good start for directing the eye, there are other ways to lead the viewer's eye through a painting. Here you'll explore different approaches for creating visual passages within a painting. Frequently, scenes you wish to paint won't offer a good visual passage. But you can always use your artistic license to create that path. To get the job done, all it takes is a little planning!

Dominance

A path or a road is a natural lead-in for the eye. But when you introduce a road into a painting, you need to consider how important you want that road to be. Is it simply going to direct the viewer's eye to a place of interest, or is it a larger part of the painting? Determining this literal path's dominance is the first step to establishing the visual path through the painting. As you look at these three examples, you'll notice that changing the viewpoint gives each a different, distinct feeling.

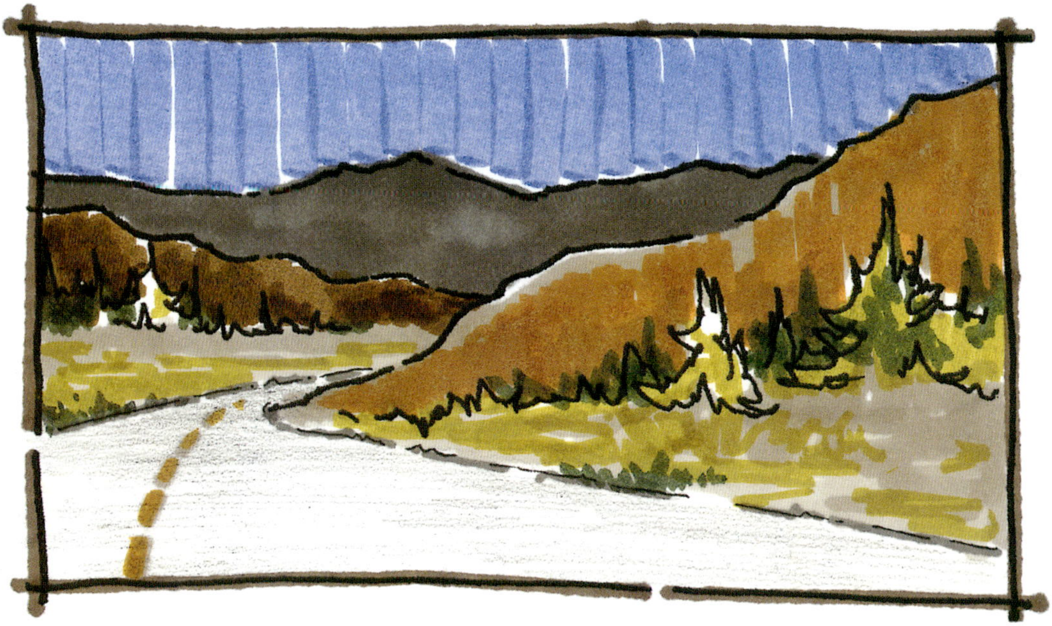

Choice One In this sketch, the road extends across the entire foreground, beyond the field of vision, making it feel as if you're on the road and have stepped into the scene. The road is the dominant element of this sketch.

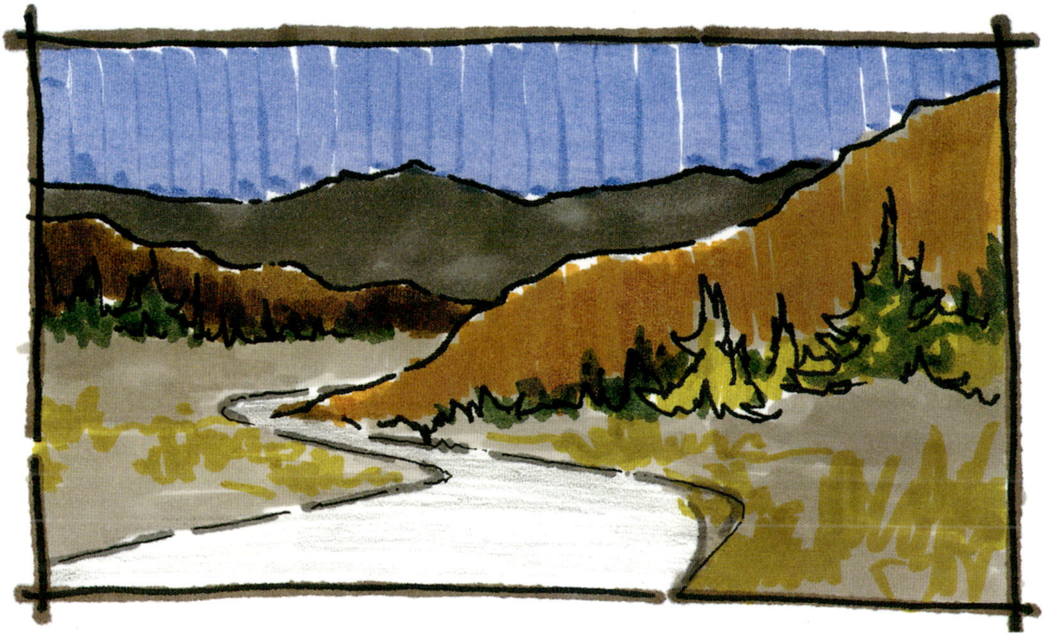

Choice Two A narrower road produces the feeling that you're viewing the road from the side. Here the road is no longer of central importance. With less prominence, the road directs the eye toward the end of the path, where it rests naturally on the mountain at the right.

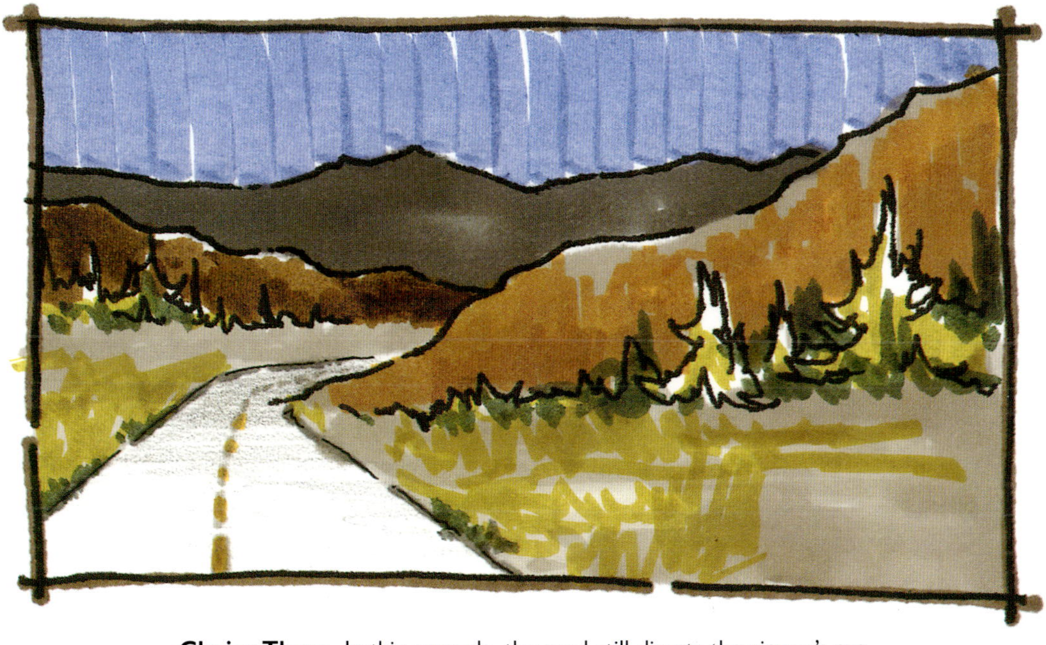

Choice Three In this example, the road still directs the viewer's eye toward the mountain to the right. But the addition of the lines in the road gives the road more dominance. Remember, detail catches the eye!

Speed

Whether you're dealing with a visual path or a literal path, its shape will determine how quickly the eye follows it—and thus how quickly the eye moves through the painting. You need to determine if you want the viewer's eye to go directly to the focal area without pause or if you want the viewer's eye to slowly make its way through the painting before resting on the center of interest. Will your path be fast or slow?

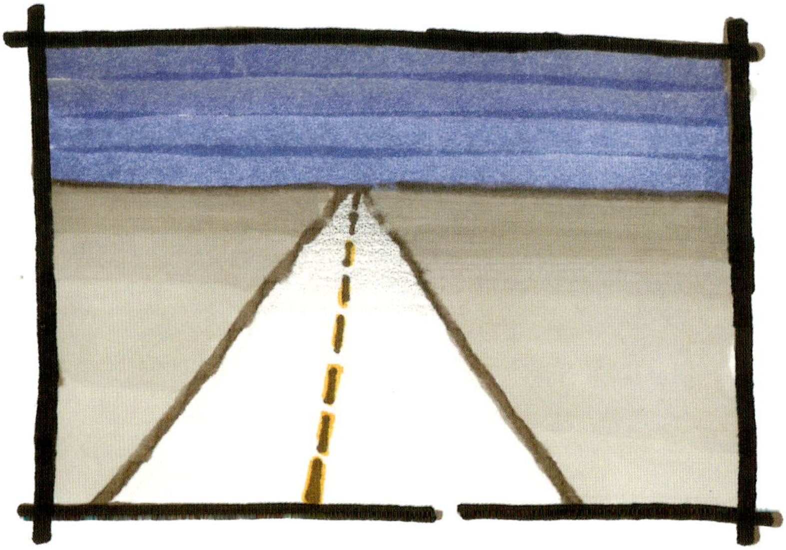

Fast Path Straight highways and sidewalks are fast paths because they have two straight lines that recede into the distance where they converge, forming an obvious path for the eye to follow.

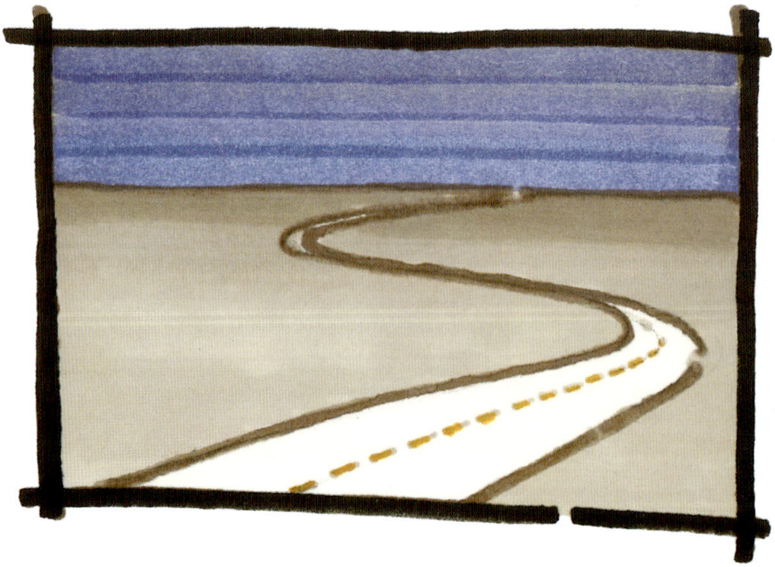

Slow Path Winding country roads and garden paths are slow paths. In these instances, the lines of the path curve, so they recede into the distance more slowly.

Open Passages

Have you ever taken an evening stroll and walked by a house with its front door open? You can't help but glance to see what's going on inside! An open door is inviting and welcoming, but it doesn't take you long to figure out that a closed door means "keep out." It works the same way with a painting. When you use a door in a painting, make it inviting and welcoming—leave the door slightly ajar or include a window in the door that can be seen through. Pique the viewer's curiosity!

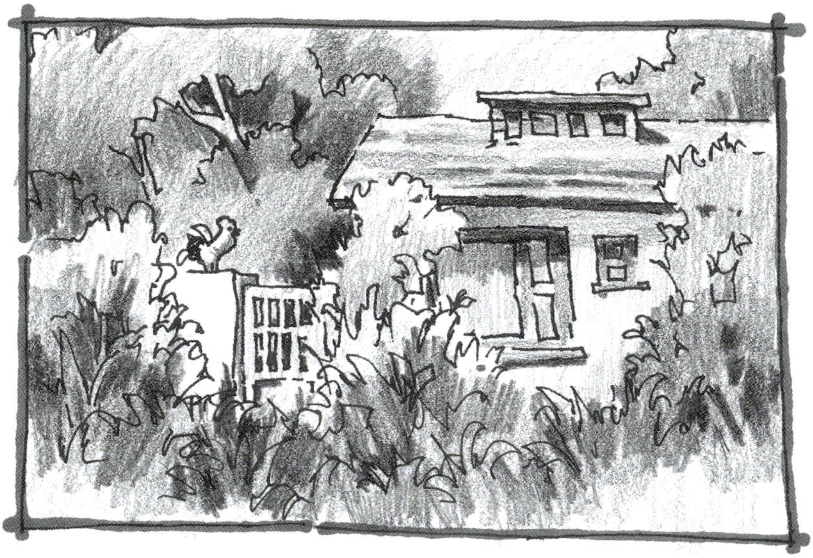

Closed Off In this study, the gate and ceramic rooster are the center of interest. The value contrasts around them help define their importance. But the foliage is so dense that it blocks the visual passage to the gate. This composition isn't working.

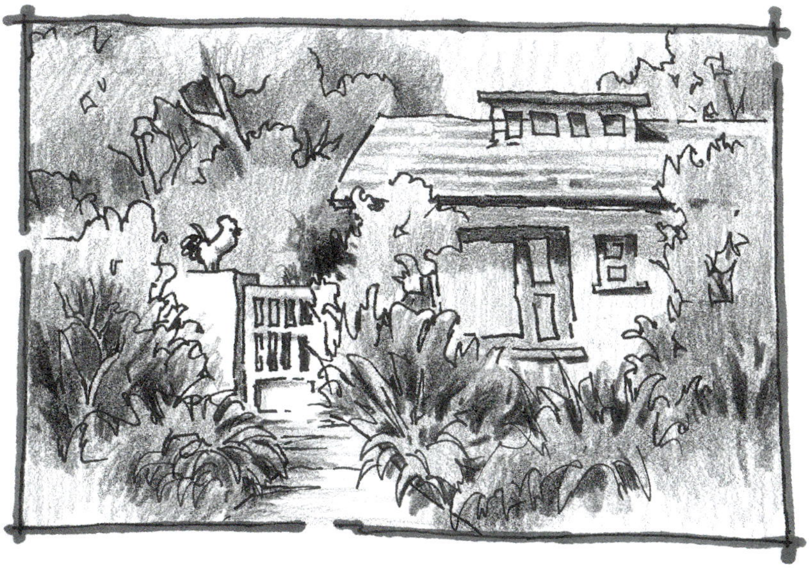

Opened Up Eliminating the foliage in front of the gate immediately opens up the area. Adding a slightly curved walkway provides a slow path for the eye.

Curving a pathway isn't the only way to slow movement. Adding shadows across the walkway will also slow down the eye.

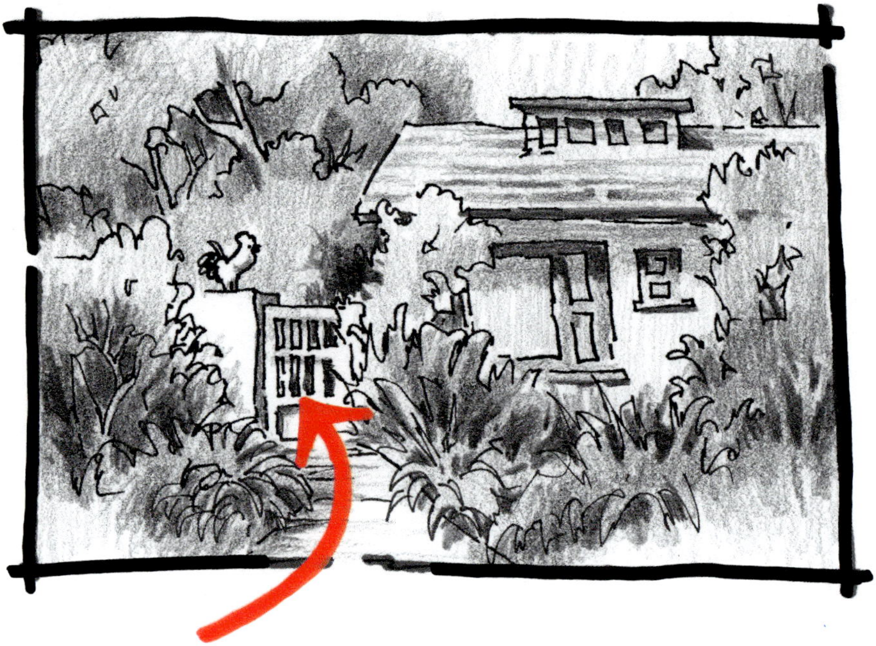

Use Value Contrasts To direct the eye up the path, keep the walkway light in value (but not as light as the focal point), and use dark values on both sides of the path to prevent the eye from straying.

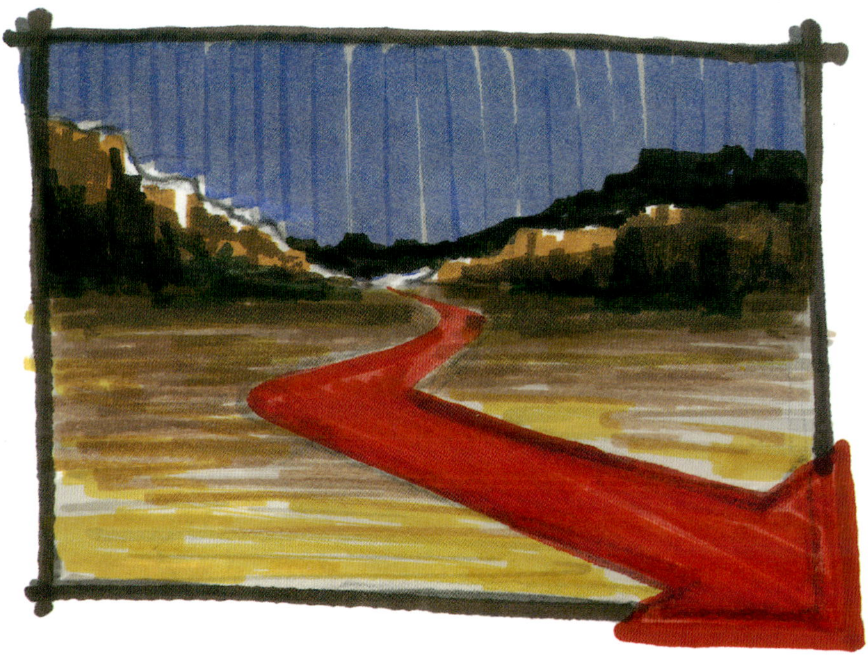

Avoid Corners Be mindful of corners when including a road or path. If a road exits on a corner, it acts as a visual arrow that directs the eye right out of the painting—not where you want it to go!

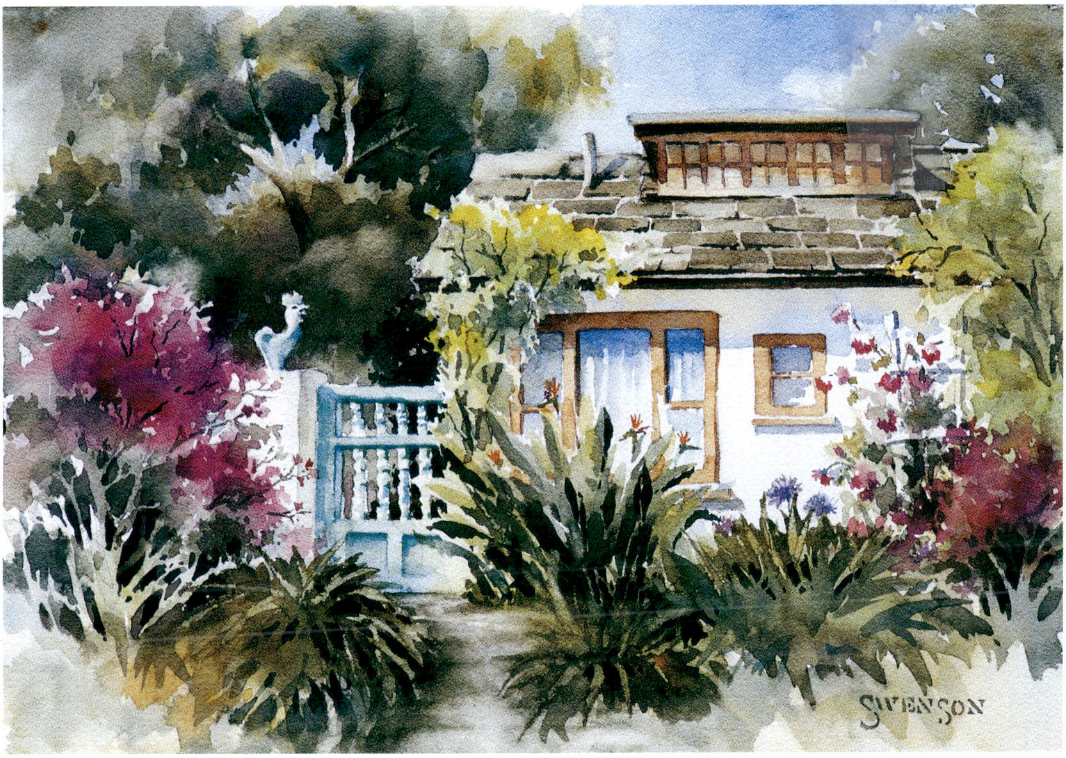

Once you've made the effort to bring the viewer's eye to a specific area, be certain it's worth looking at! In the reference photo, there was very little contrast among colors or values. In the final painting, contrasting warm pink bougainvilleas against cool green trees helps accentuate the focal point. Now the greatest amount of both detail and contrast resides in this area.

Zooming In on Details

When working from a reference photo, sometimes the detail can be hard to see. This is where a computer comes in very handy! You can crop the photo to focus on the area of interest and then print out the altered image at a more appropriate size for reference.

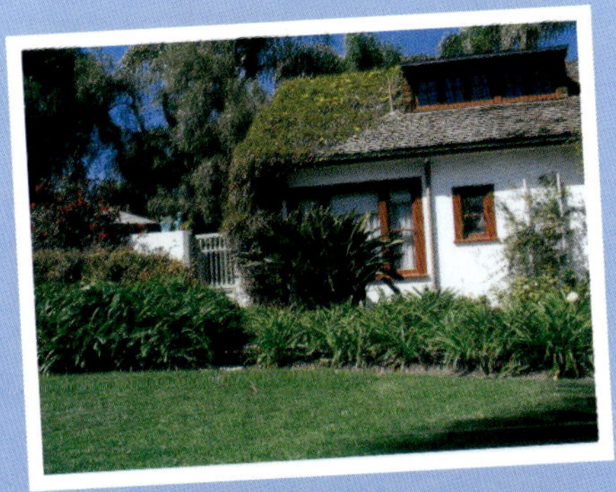

◀ **Too Small** The rooster and gate are the center of interest—but they're so small in the original photo, you can hardly make them out.

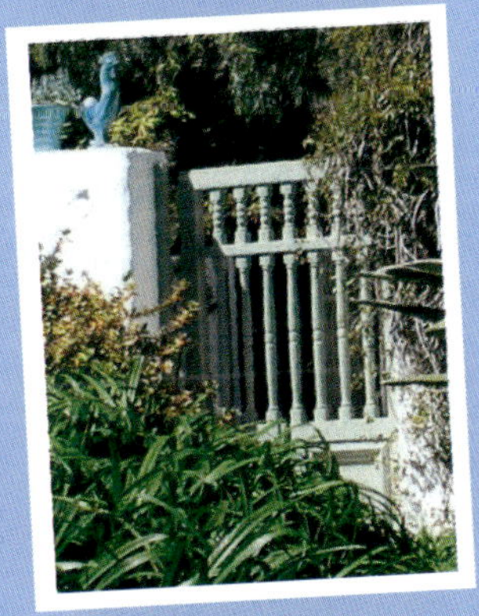

▶ **Just Right** The solution? Crop the original photo, and print a new image at a size you'll be comfortable using. Much better!

Step Six: Vary Edges

Not only is variety the spice of life, it's also the spice of painting! So it should come as no surprise that the most interesting paintings have varied edges. A painting done completely wet into wet will have all soft edges, resulting in a mushy look without any focus. And a painting with only hard edges will be busy and sharp, making it difficult to look at. Combining all different kinds of edges—even textured and lost edges—not only gives depth, focus, and interest to the subject matter, but it also gives the viewers more enjoyment because it encourages them to actively participate in the painting, allowing their minds to complete the missing details where you've incorporated soft or lost edges. Varying edges produces a finished piece that is both more realistic and more interesting.

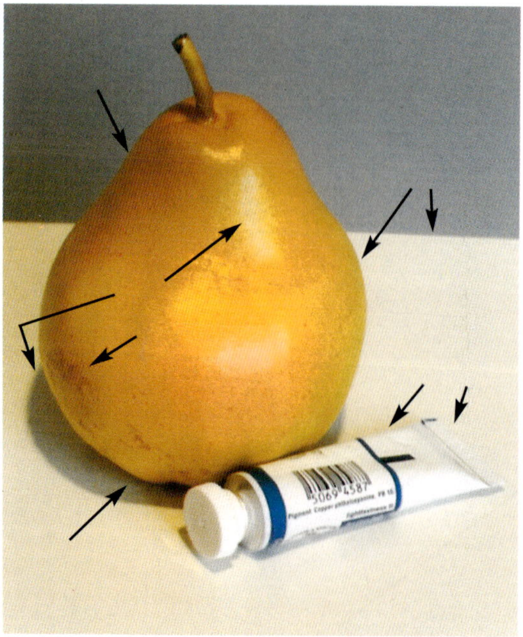

Distinguishing Edge Types Varied edges aren't limited to painting—they're a part of life. In this photo, you can pick out hard edges, soft edges, and even *lost edges* (where an edge merges with an adjacent edge).

◀ **Hard** Hard edges suggest structural, angular, and mechanical subjects. Their sharpness attracts more attention than other edges, so save them for the focal area. To make a hard edge, apply wet paint to dry paper.

▶ **Soft** Soft edges produce rounded, soft, distant, and diffused areas. They shouldn't be used for your primary focus. For soft edges, paint wet into wet, soften a freshly painted edge with clean water, or lift out color.

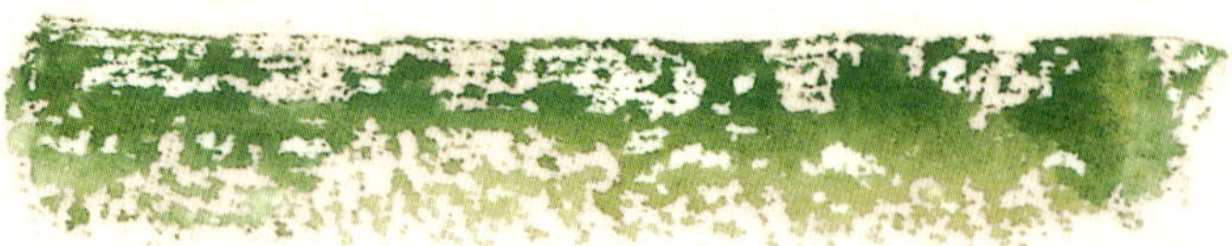

◀ **Textured** These broken edges define rough objects like wood, and they can be used anywhere. Create them by dragging a lot of paint and minimal water across the paper with a brush.

Experimenting with Edges

Take a closer look at the pear and paint tube to understand the way edges work. Improper use can detract from your painting. But properly applied edges will enhance even the simplest of subjects!

Hard Edges Here the subject is painted with hard edges only. The feeling is stiff and illustrative, not painterly. If your subject appears to have all hard edges, remove your glasses, squint a little, or even use your computer to blur the image a bit.

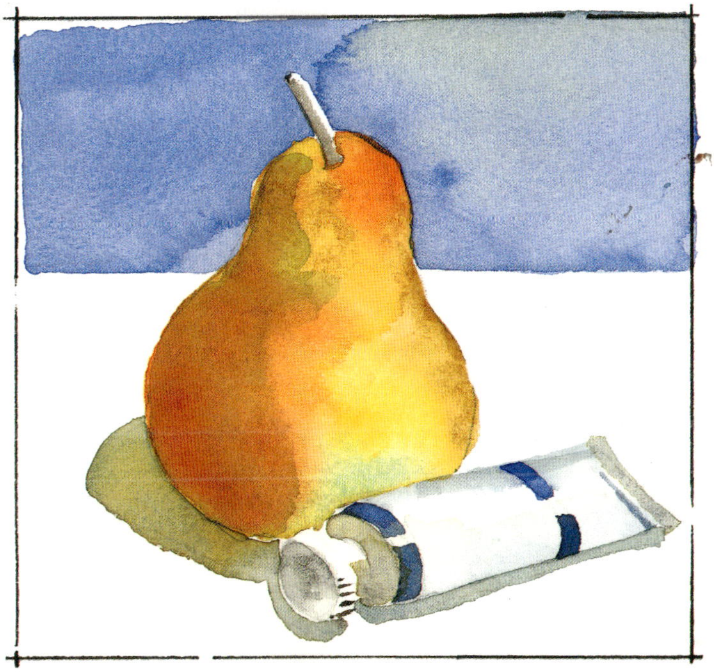

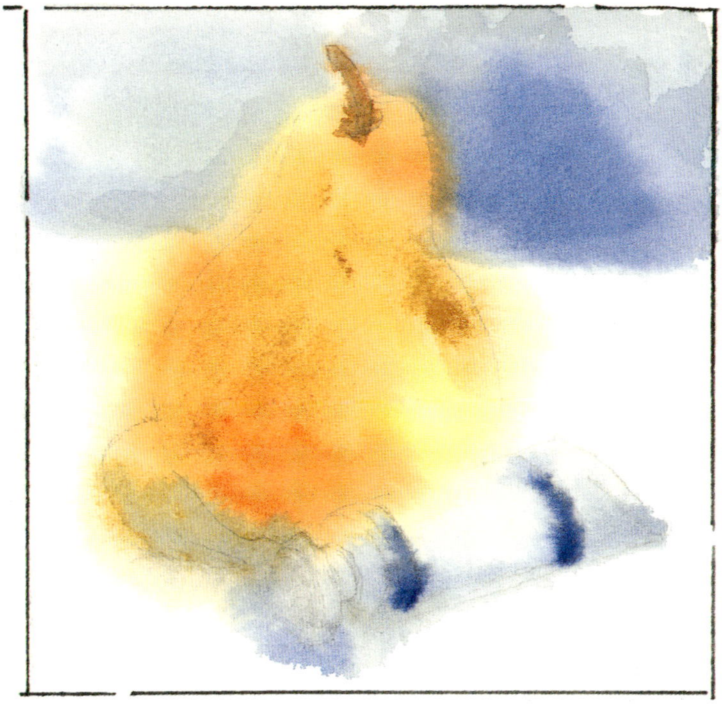

Soft Edges This second study is painted completely wet into wet, resulting in soggy-looking soft edges without any strength.

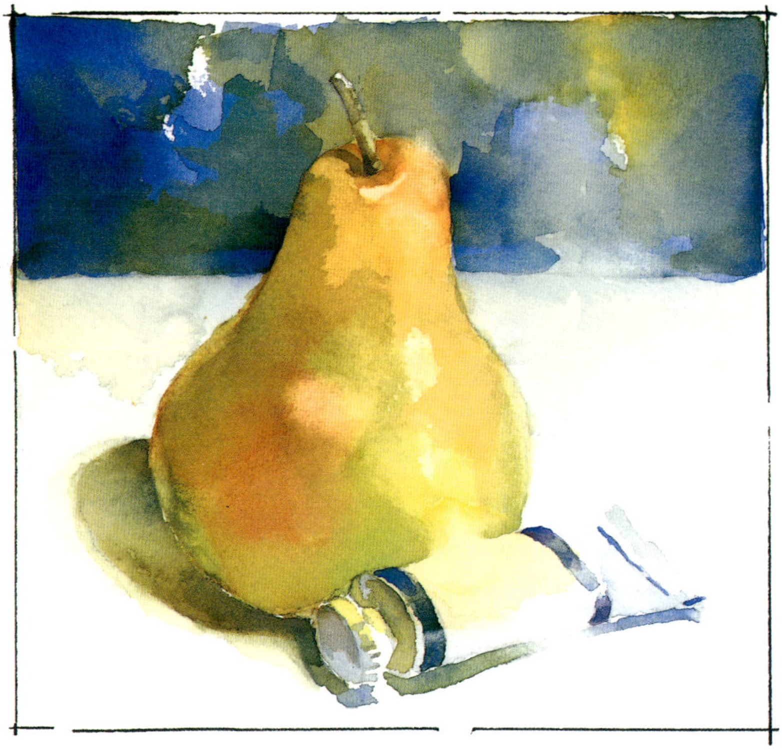

Varied Edges This study is an improvement upon the others. The subject looks more lively because the painting includes a combination of hard edges, soft edges, and lost edges. Find the edges yourself. (They've changed a bit from the photo! Remember, the eye sees differently than the camera does.)

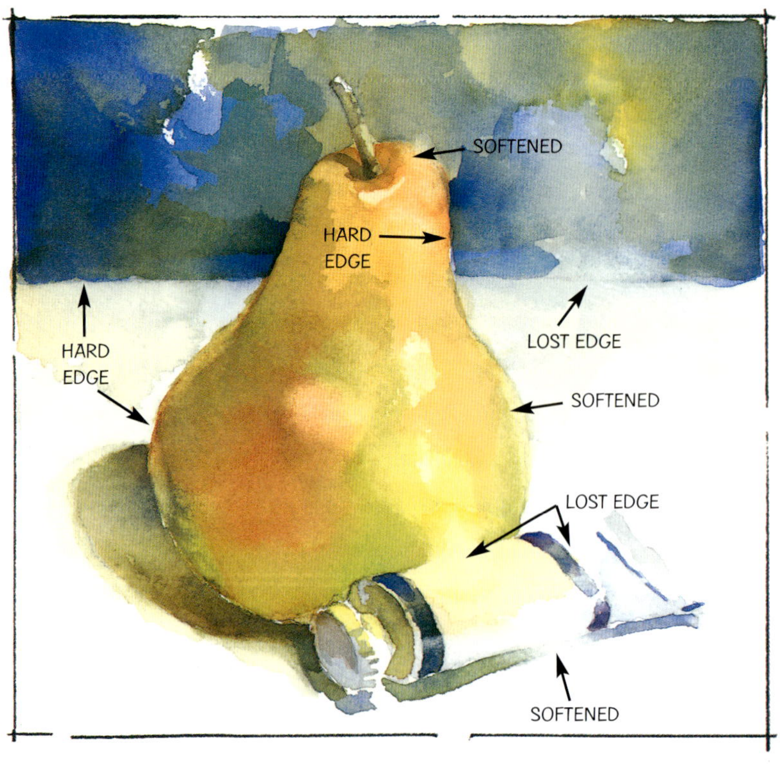

Edges Revealed How did you do? The white tube of paint is on a white surface, which allows for many lost edges. The pear is a little more difficult because you don't see the lost edges right away. When you have two areas that are close in value, squint and you'll see that the edge disappears. Once you can begin to identify various types of edges, it will be easier for you to create them.

Approaching Different Subjects

The same edge principles apply to every subject you might wish to paint. But human figures present a special challenge: They can make a simple concept difficult because we have expectations about what we will see. In reality, creating a realistic portrait is no more difficult than painting a simple still life; it's simply a matter of careful observation.

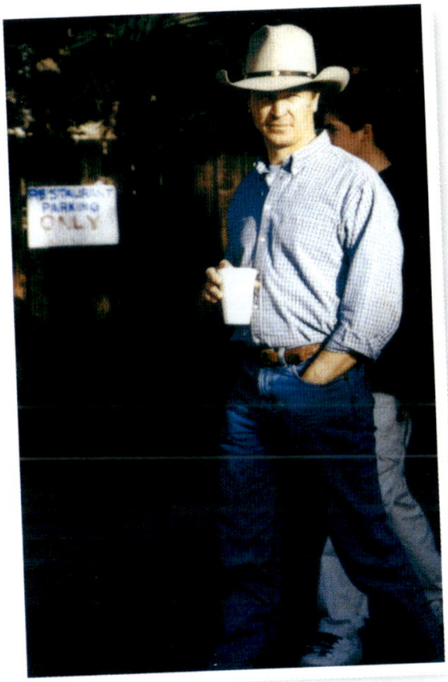

Shadows and Edges

Before you begin identifying the edges in a more complex subject, it's helpful to first delineate the shadows. Subjects that have strong contrast between light and shadow areas are best to work with because the shadow shapes will be strong and more exciting. And where the shadows and light intermingle, there will be hard edges, soft edges, and areas where the two types of edges meet—in other words, variety!

Original Photo The lighting of this photo results in a range of light and dark values, soft and hard edges, and warm and cool tones across the subject's face. It would make a great reference—except the face is about 1/2" tall! Avoid working from photos this small—if you're not careful, you'll spend more time looking at the photo than painting.

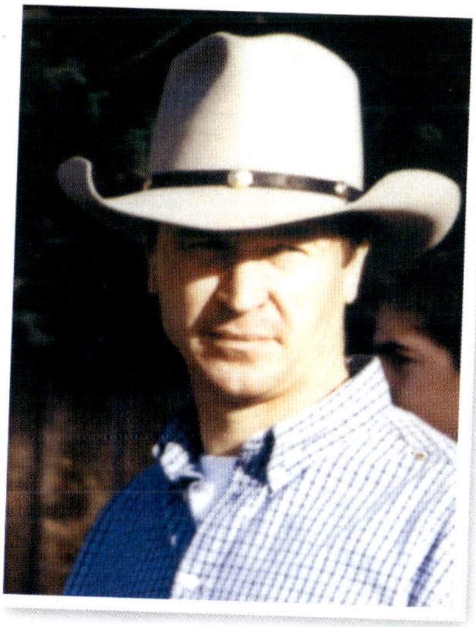

Cropped Photo The strong pattern of light made it worthwhile to scan the photo into my computer, crop it, and print it at a larger size. Now you can see the shadows and edges much more clearly.

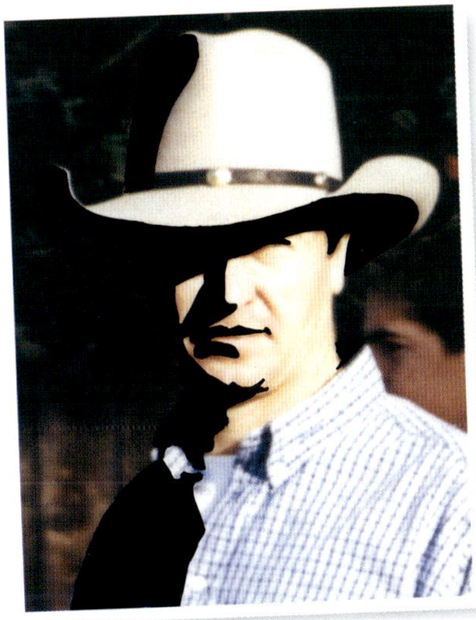

Emphasizing the Shadows Use a black marker to fill in the shadows so you can distinctly see their shapes. And be sure to notice the way the shadows merge into one another, regardless of edge type.

Final Planning

When you first begin to draw or paint, it's tempting to try to record everything you see. But it's possible to see too much! When it comes time to paint, stop studying your original reference and start relying on pencil studies for design, value placement, and edge location. This way you'll focus on the important elements, without trying to include every minute detail your eye can perceive.

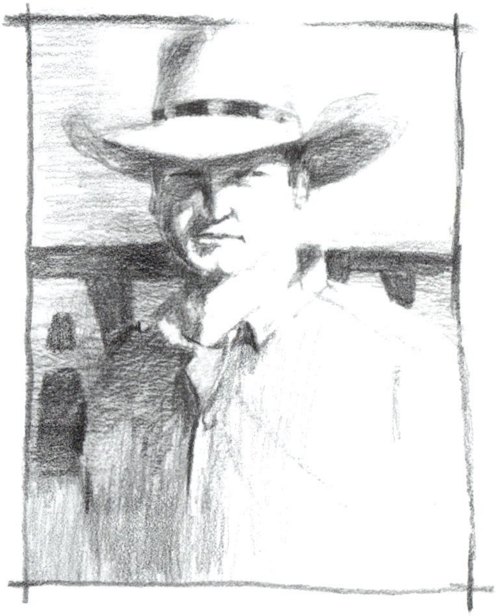

Value Study Carefully study your photo reference for edges, paying special attention to the types of edges the shadows create. Cast shadows will have a hard edge—for these areas, apply a dark value. Form shadows will have a soft edge—as they turn toward the light source, apply a light value. When you see areas that are close in value, merge them in your sketch. When it's complete, use your value study as your painting reference, putting the photo aside.

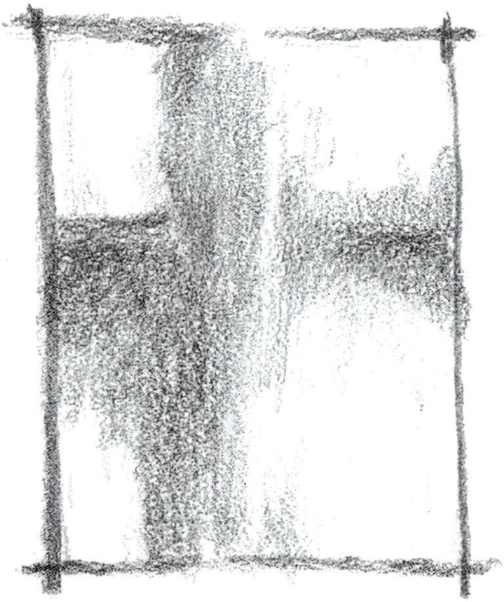

Cruciform Design The shadows and value placement suggest a cruciform design. You may have already noticed the sign in the value study; it provides a balancing horizontal thrust.

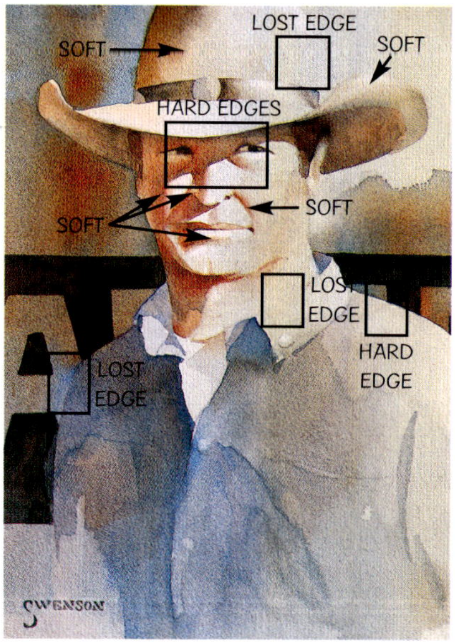

Cheat Sheet Notice the way the pencil study mapping transfers to the finished painting. For example, a soft edge along the jaw starts as a light pencil line and becomes an area of lifted color.

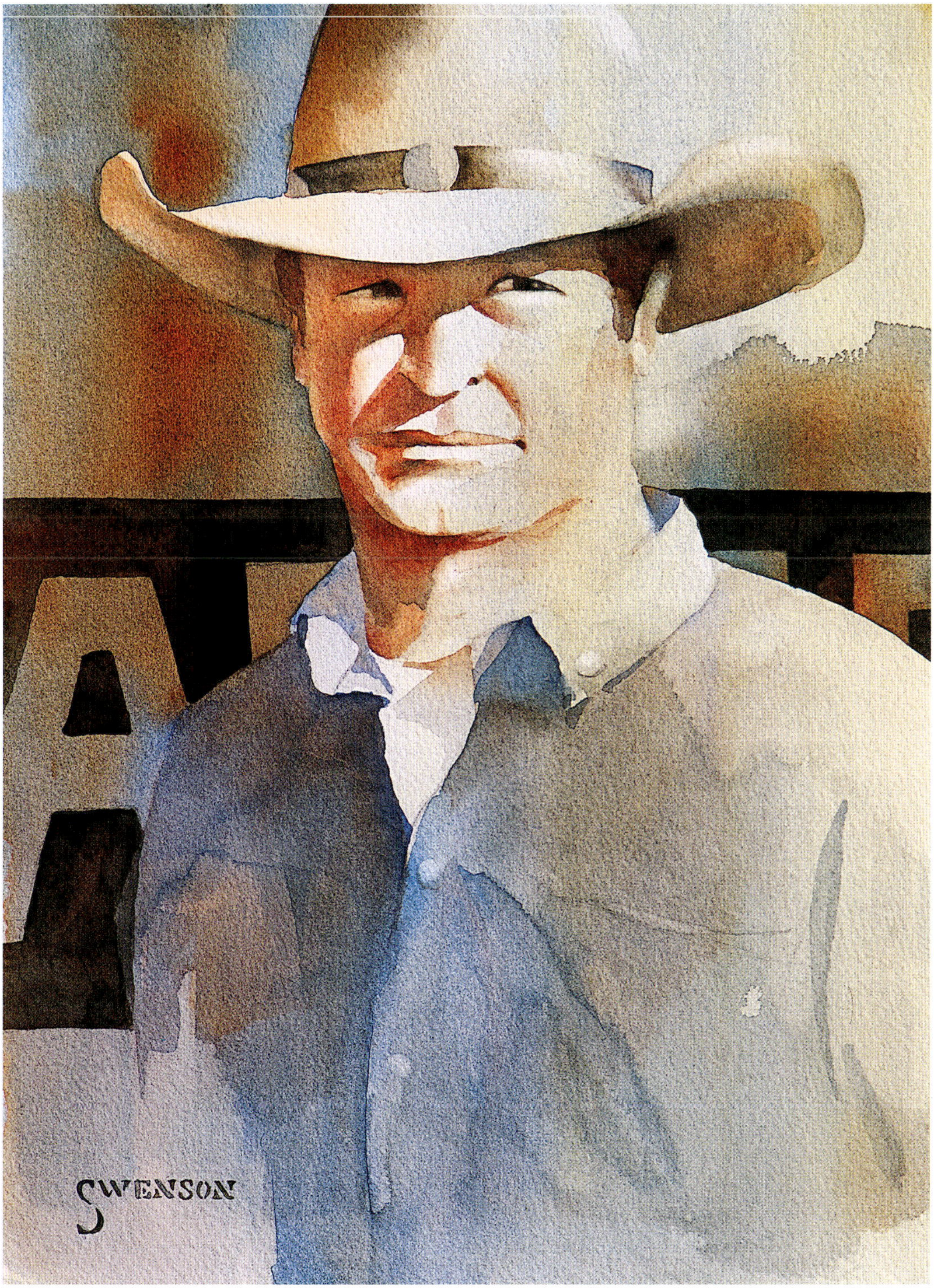

Hard edges, soft edges, lost edges . . . Did you notice anything missing from this painting? There are no rough edges. And that is perfectly okay! You don't need to use every technique you know in every painting, just as long as there is variety.

Step Seven: Enrich Lights and Shadows

When assessing a subject or scene, look for the presence of light and how it affects the subject. Light is responsible for revealing form, color, and texture—and it can transform an ordinary scene into something dramatic, exciting, and full of life! Where there is light, you'll also find shadows. Contrary to popular belief, shadows aren't all dark, gray, and dingy—in fact, it's in shadows where you, the artist, will find the greatest possibilities for exciting color.

Cast and Form Shadows

Not all shadows are alike. There are two very distinct kinds of shadows that occur in any subject: cast shadows and form shadows. Recognizing these and approaching them differently will improve your paintings. So what are the differences?

When we think of shadows, usually we think of cast shadows. *Cast shadows* result when an object blocks the light source. These shadows mimic the shape of the object that casts them and usually have hard edges. On the other hand, *form shadows* are shadows on the parts of an object facing away from the light source. Form shadows are lighter in value and have softer edges. But shadows don't have the same value and edges all over. Cast shadows become paler, warmer, and softer as they recede from the object casting them. And form shadows also change according to their location—the palest, warmest, and softest parts of these shadows are located nearest the light source.

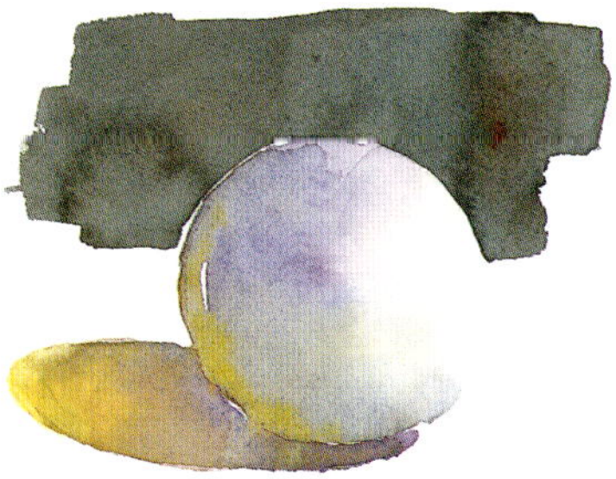

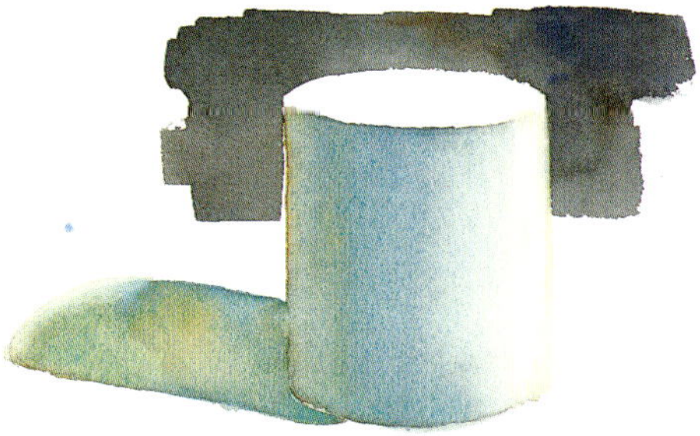

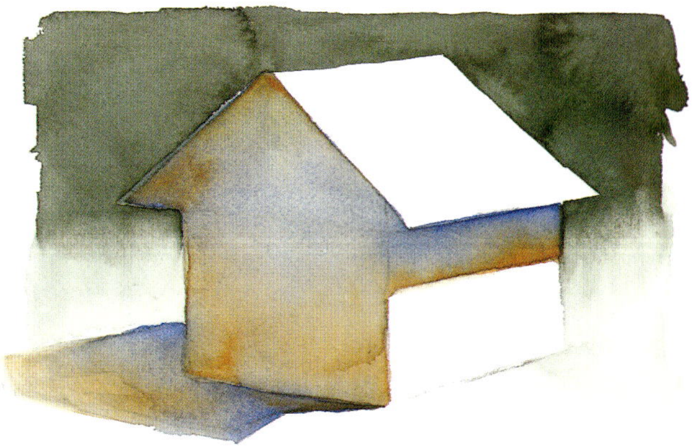

Grounding with Shadows Form shadows are responsible for making ordinary, flat shapes (such as the subjects of a drawing or painting) appear three-dimensional. In addition to providing a sense of dimension, shadows ground the object in space, so it doesn't appear to be floating in air. Paint cast shadows that are darkest near the object and gradually lighten with distance to produce a subject that appears natural and true to life—resulting in a ball rather than a circle, a cylinder rather than a rectangle, and a house rather than a polygon.

Reflected Light

Students will often reach for a tube of gray when preparing to paint shadows. What they don't know is that shadows contain reflections from the illuminated areas near them—this *reflected light* carries color into the shadows. And it's not just the shadows that contain reflected light! All parts of an object that aren't directly in the path of the light source are affected by reflected light and the color carried within. In the images below, the buildings contain hints of the colored grounds, especially in the cast and form shadows that are present. Take a closer look!

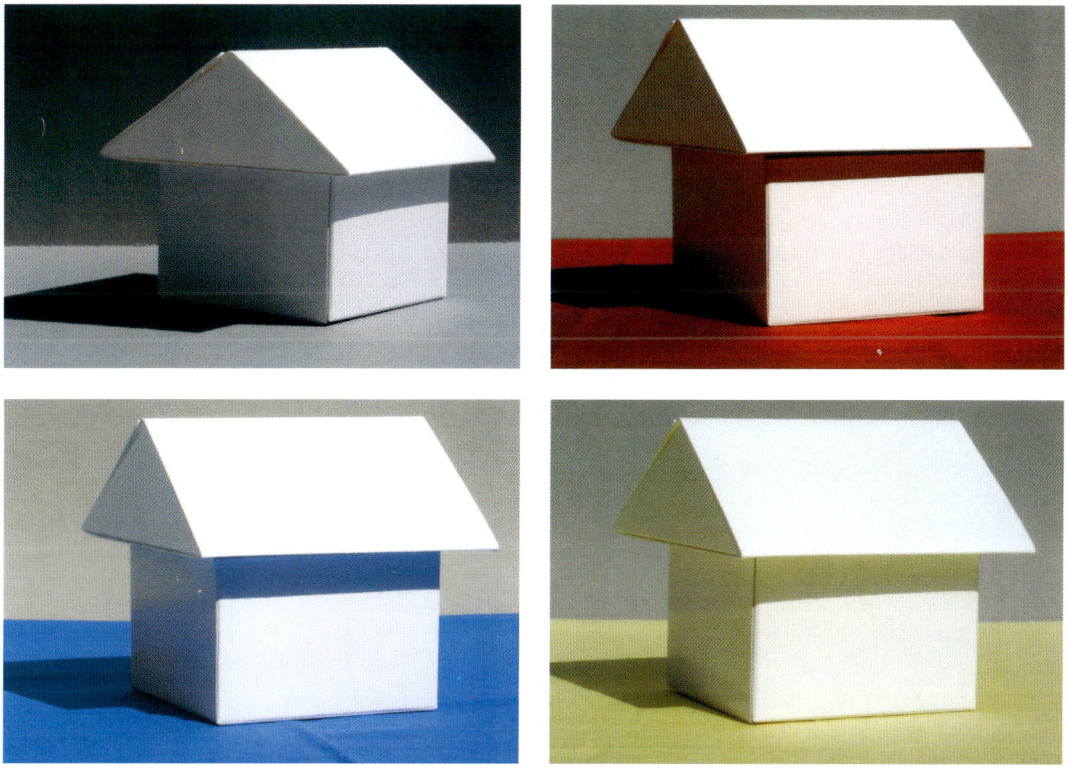

Shadows and Shape Reflected light is easier to understand when you can actually see it happen. The general shape of a building demonstrates this point. In the first example, you'll notice that the shadows are indeed gray—because the object is placed on a gray surface! But place the same structure on different colored surfaces and watch what happens! In each example, the shadows change color as they appear in different areas around the building, becoming richer and darker as they move away from the light source. The reflected light changes with different colored surfaces—for instance, the reflected light on the side of the building is less evident in the yellow example than in the red or the blue examples—but the yellow is definitely still present in the shadows.

"Don't be afraid of color; it makes painting rich."
–Millard Sheets

Changing Light

When looking for subject matter outdoors, be mindful of the changing light. Make it a point to know which direction the sun is moving. An object might appear drab and dull one moment, but it can become an ideal painting subject a few minutes later; it all depends on the angle of the sun. Observe objects at different times of day to get a feel for the effect of the sun. In the early morning, shadows are long and cool. By midday, the high sun eliminates most shadows (and thus most interest). By late afternoon, shadows grow long again—and this time they're enriched with warm colors.

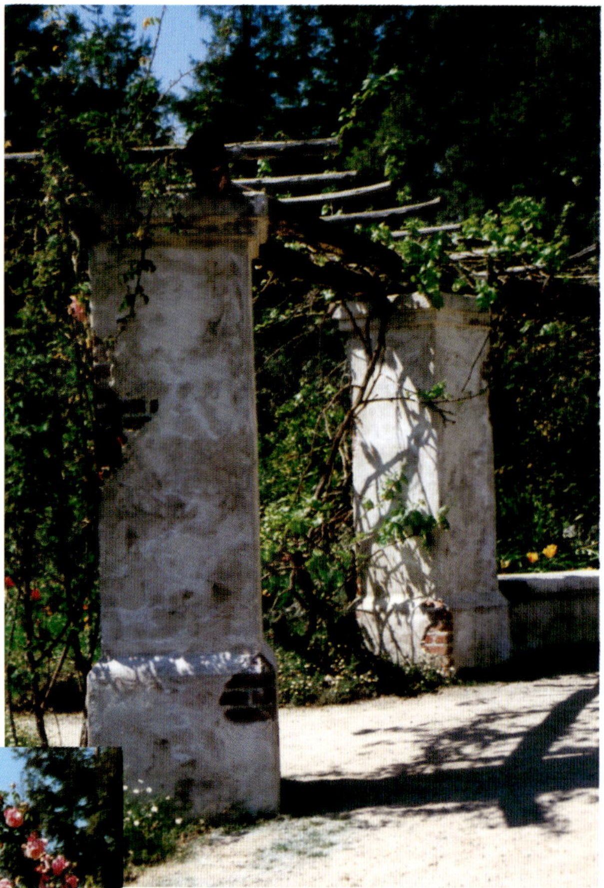

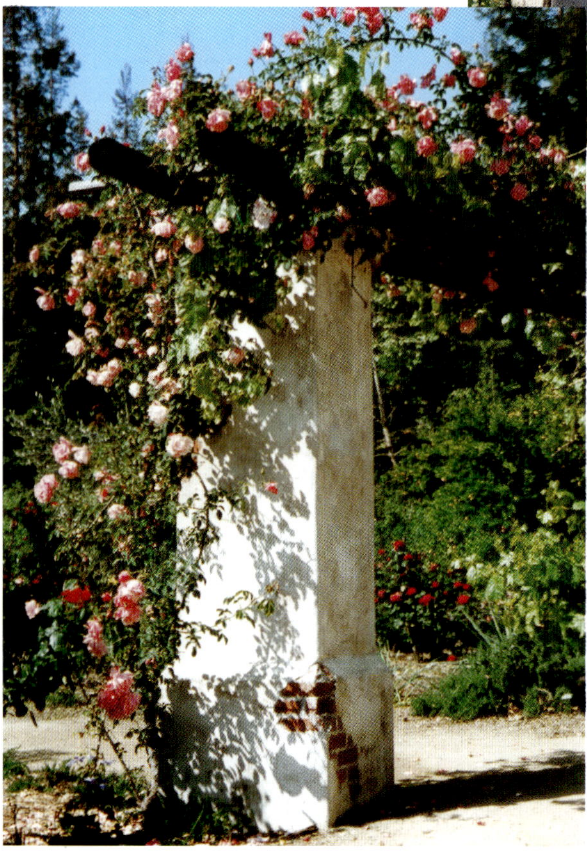

▲ **Shadowed Subject** In this photo, taken in the early morning, the long, cool shadows are overwhelming the little bits of sunlight that are filtering through the foliage. A little more sunshine would help this scene immensely—in time, the shadows will shorten as the sun rises, so it's simply a matter of waiting!

◀ **Sunlit Subject** A bit later in the morning, the shadows begin to recede. Earlier the pillar was draped in shadow, but now you can pick out the shapes of the vines in the shadows they cast on the pillar. It's the interplay of light and shadow—the contrast and variation in values and the formation of interesting shapes—that creates the drama. These aspects of the scene will disappear when they are flooded with light at noon.

Making Shadows Work for You

When you're looking for a subject to paint, don't discard ordinary, everyday objects. The ground alone may seem unworthy of a painting—but it takes on an entirely different aspect when you see it dappled with interesting patterns of sunlight that has filtered through the leaves of a tree. Objects can appear transformed by light filtering through blinds, reflected by a pool, or partially blocked by twisting vines. Keep your eyes and your mind open to possibility!

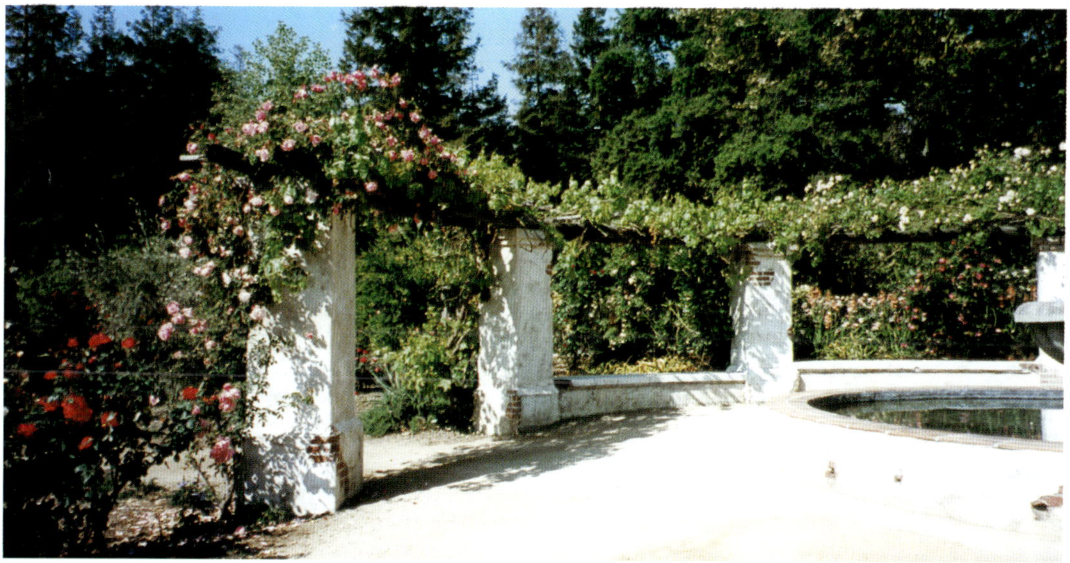

Transforming a Simple Scene Pillars alone are a very simple subject, but the vines that top these make them more interesting—especially when the light hits the vines in such a way that they cast intricate shadows on the ground and pillars. Here you'll find interesting shapes and a good balance between light and dark!

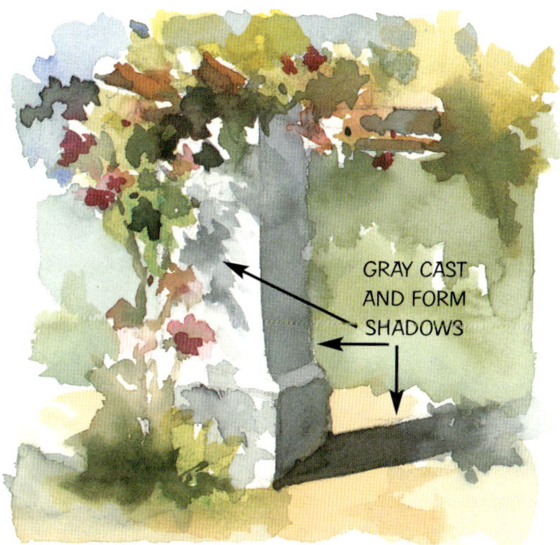

Photos have a tendency to make shadows appear darker than they are in reality—and delicate hints of reflected color are usually nonexistent. Observe shadows and reflected light from life when you can. There is no better teacher than your own observation!

Gray Shadows If you copied from the photo directly, it would be easy to mistake the shadows for gray. But look at how your painting would turn out. You already know to include reflective light in shadows—so no matter what you think you see in a reference, don't be led astray!

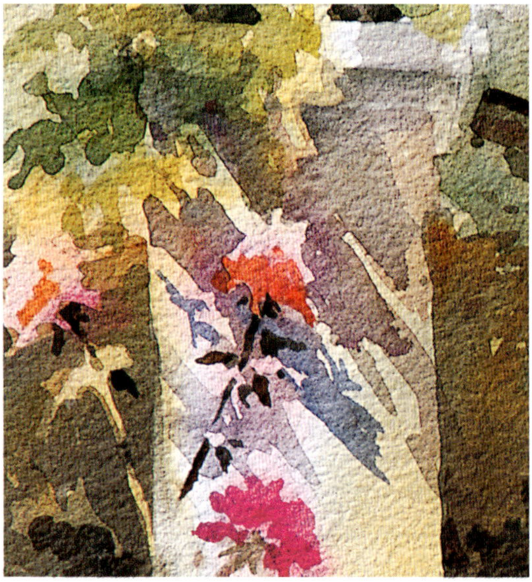

◀ **Reflected Light in Shadows** The real key to making this subject interesting is to include plenty of color. Start with the reflected light: The shadows at the top of the pillar contain some beautiful shades of pink reflected by the neighboring flowers. Emphasizing color is a great way to add vitality to your painting.

▼ **Cast Shadows** Remember that the cast shadows are darker and have harder edges than the form shadows, but they also contain reflected light and color.

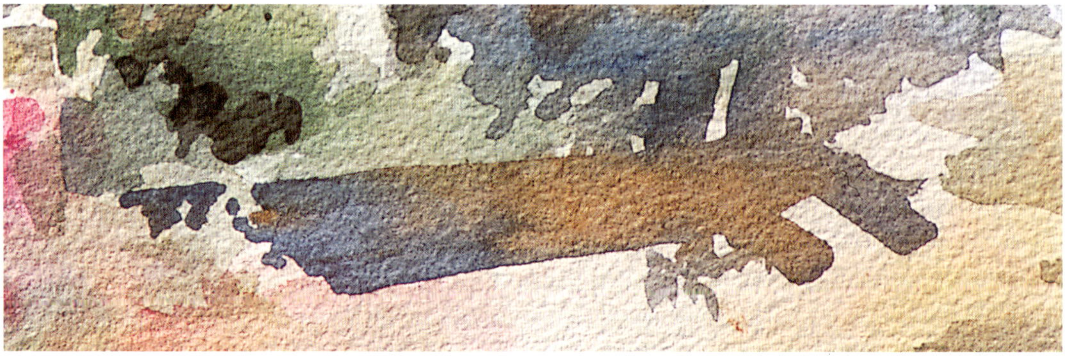

▶ **Form Shadows** Don't make the mistake of creating solid form shadows. There should be a fair amount of variation in the intensity and tone of the shadows, as shown here. Notice the way that the colors of the shadows are all slightly different throughout the painting, as each shadow contains reflected light that is dependent upon what is nearby.

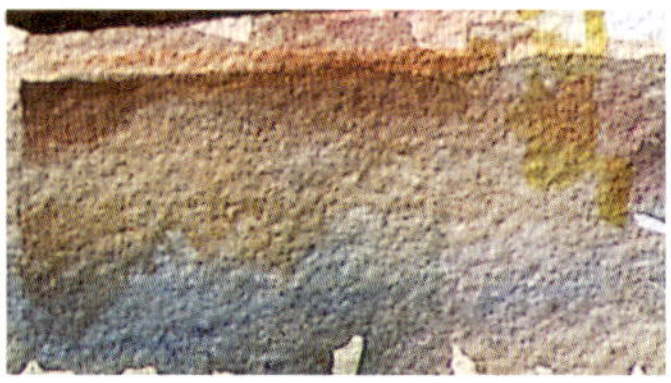

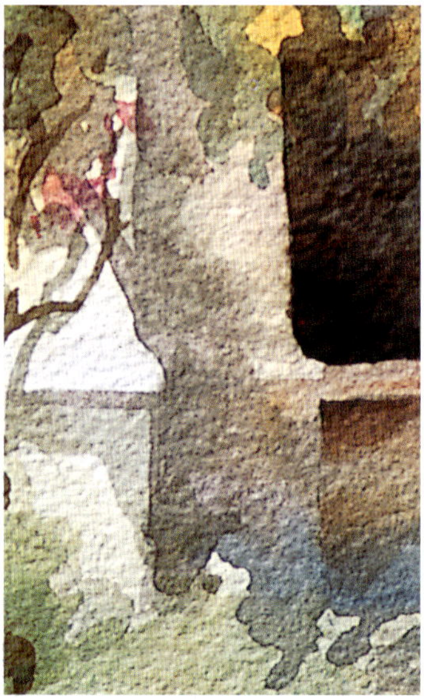

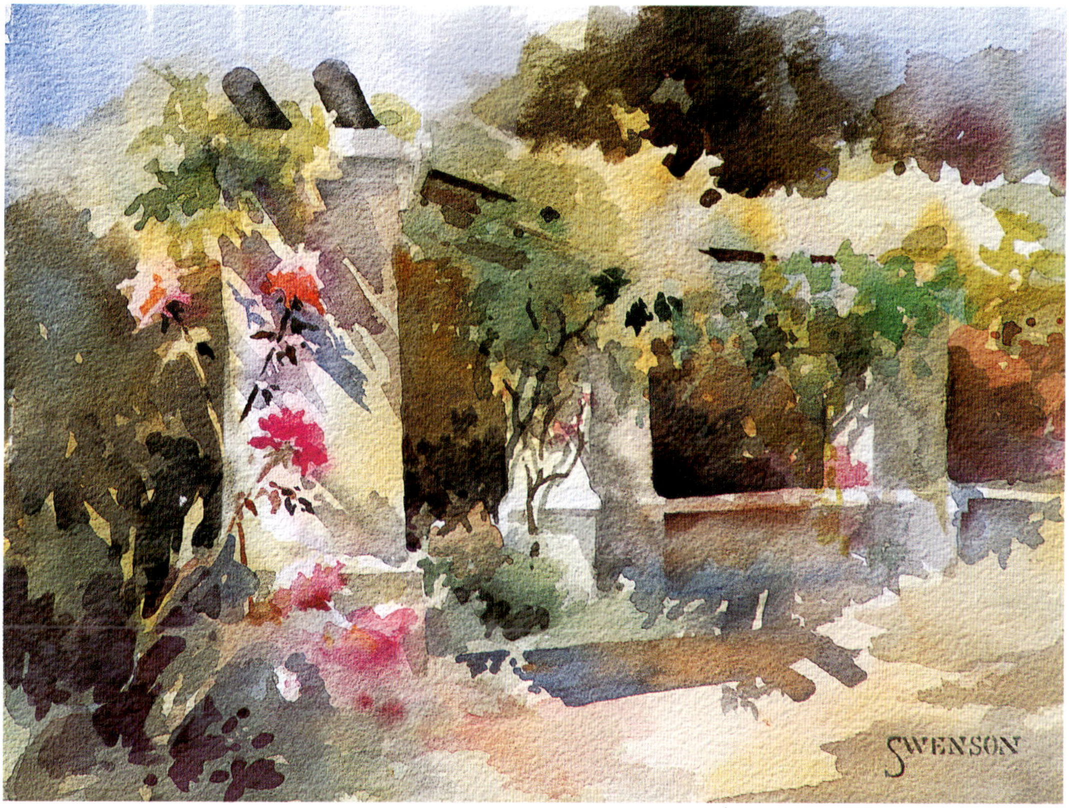

Colorful shadows build drama and excitement in this painting. Use your artistic license to emphasize the colors you see—regardless of what your photo reference reveals. What makes a painting beautiful is the way you, the artist, influence the scene, not how closely the finished piece resembles the initial reference.

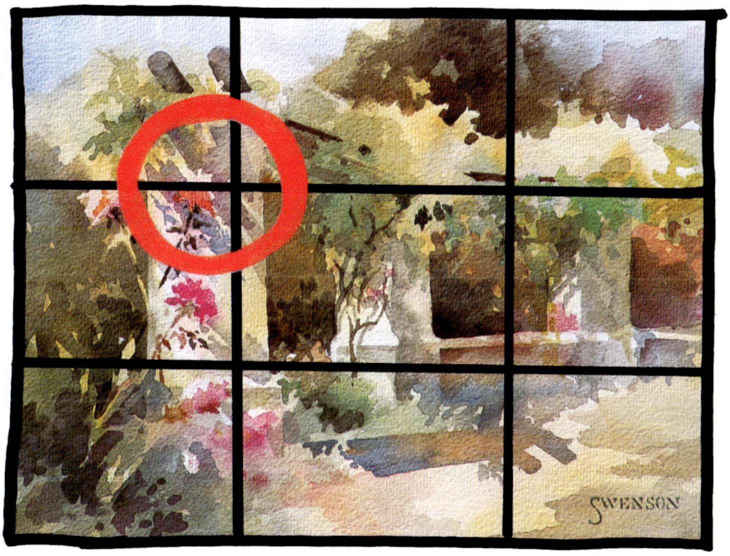

Center of Interest It's no coincidence that the bright pink color within the cast shadows draws attention to the column on the far left. The bright, intense color in this area highlights the center of interest—the result of careful planning!

Step Eight: Maximize the Effect of White

Artists who paint in other media have the advantage of adding white highlights with paint at any stage of development, but .with transparent watercolor, the artist's paper becomes the white. This means you must preserve the precious white and light values of the paper from the start. You can do so much more than just save your whites, though—there are many ways to enhance your whites to make them truly sing!

When you paint the space around an object, you are painting the negative shapes. The term "negative painting" often puts people off. It definitely sounds like something unpleasant; however, it is one of the most exciting approaches to painting! And it's an essential technique when working with a white subject in a painting.

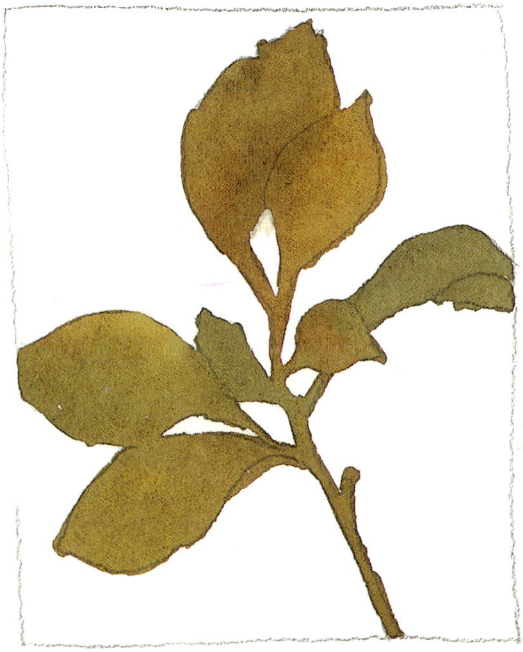

Positive Painting In most instances, painters work in a "positive" manner—in other words, they simply paint the object they see by filling in its shape, using a direct, straightforward approach.

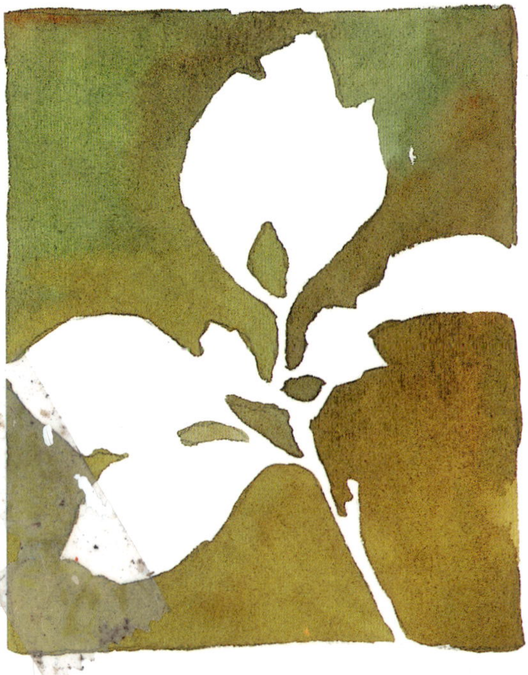

Alternative Approach But what happens when your subject is white? You can't paint the object itself, so you must paint around it to define its shape. What you don't paint stands out the most!

"The painting is usually finished before you are."
—Rex Brandt

Negative Painting

One way to save the white of the paper is by masking. But masking your whites can produce hard, unnatural edges, and you've already learned how important varied edges are! So how, exactly, should you go about negative painting without masking? Let me show you. . . .

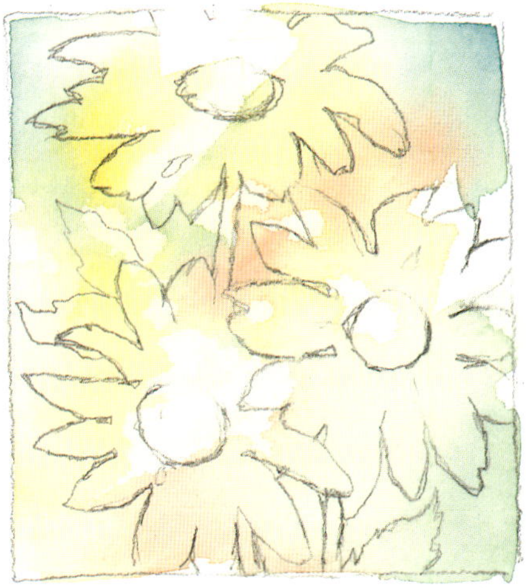

Step One Just as shadows contain hints of reflected colors, so do whites—and adding those colors makes white objects glow. So begin negative painting with a wet-into-wet underpainting that overlaps the flower petals.

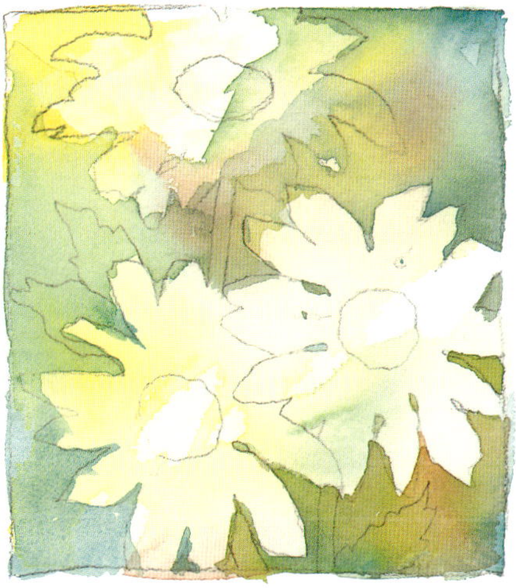

Step Two When the underpainting is dry, glaze over the negative area at the flowers' edges, pulling the color toward the paper's edges and diluting the wash as you move away from the focal area. A strong contrast near the flowers helps them pop.

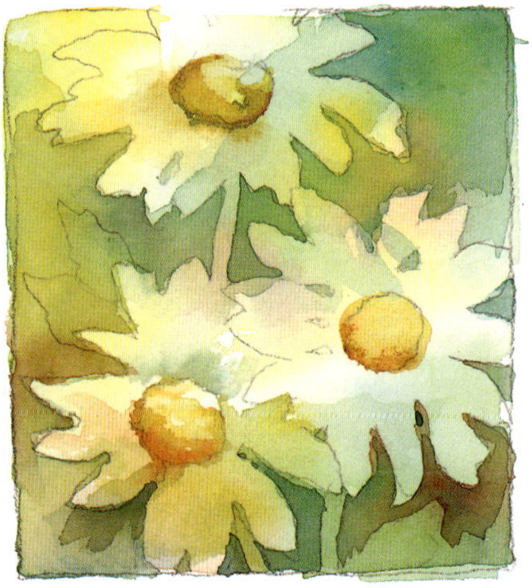

Step Three You'll still need to build up the negative shapes more for contrast and definition, but first concentrate on making the whites glow. After filling the centers of the flowers, cover the background and portions of the flowers with a glaze.

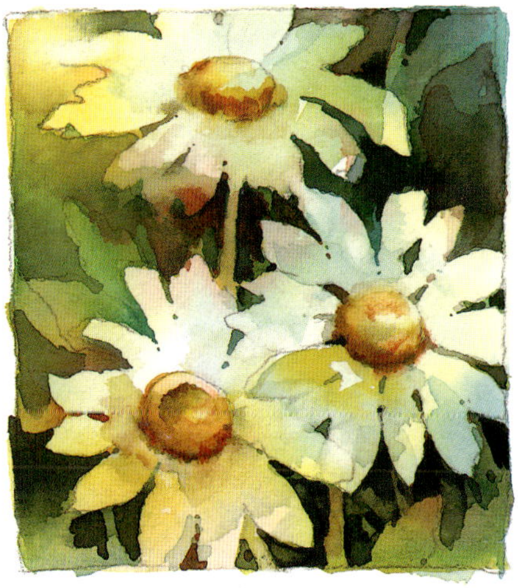

Step Four Apply the darkest glaze, selectively placing the darks to contrast against areas where you want the eye to look. Small negative shapes define the highlights near the center; darker negative spaces in the background suggest stems and leaves.

Glowing Whites

As the daisies on the previous page demonstrate, rarely do you come across an object that is entirely white. A pure white object would look flat and cut out because it would have no form. Regardless of an object's color (or lack thereof), when something turns away from a light source, it will have a form shadow. In this shadow, you'll see reflected color from nearby objects. So adding gentle hints of color to a white object not only gives it a glow, but it also produces a sense of dimension and life!

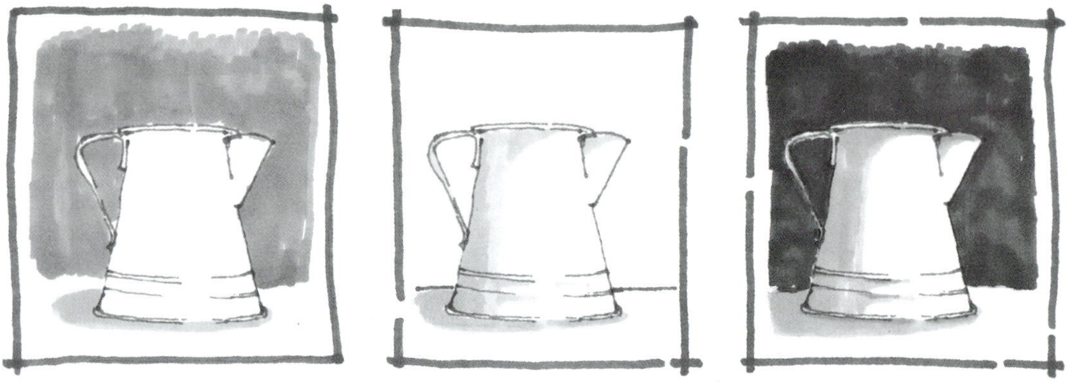

Making Whites Stand Out In the first sketch, the white pitcher is placed against a medium-value background, and it's grounded in the scene with a cast shadow. But the result is somewhat flat and uninteresting; the pitcher has no form shadows and the background doesn't offer enough contrast, so the pitcher appears to be cut out. In the second image, the pitcher has form shadows that should give it definition and interest—but because the white object is set against a white background, there isn't a real sense of dimension. In the third image, the form shadows, combined with the dark, contrasting background, give the white pitcher a feeling of form and mass. The whites really stand out!

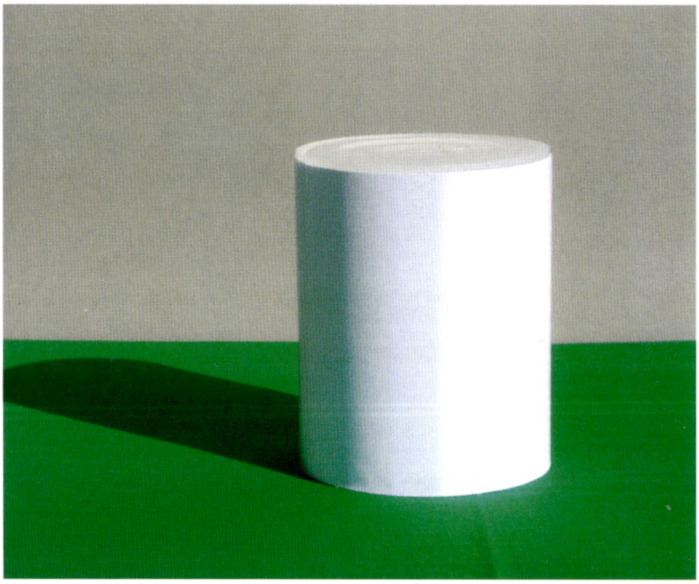

When White Isn't White White objects are white only where they are in direct light. Otherwise, white objects are colored by the reflected light from surrounding objects. In the form shadows, the whites will glow with hints of the surrounding color, as you can see in the green form shadows on this white cylinder.

Combining Concepts

Most white subjects don't stand alone—they usually are one element in a scene with other objects of many colors—some lighter in value, some darker. This means that you'll need to use a combined approach of positive and negative painting to create the finished piece. Don't worry, it's not hard—like everything you've accomplished so far, it just requires a little planning.

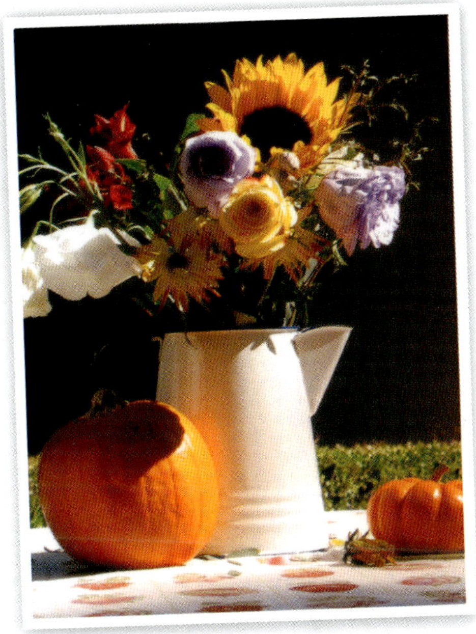

▶ **Assessing the Subject** This still life setup incorporates a pitcher with hard edges that will require a slightly different approach than the soft edges of the flower petals in the negative painting demonstration on page 53. You'll still need to paint the negative shapes to define the pitcher's shape, but you can't be quite as loose with the overlapping washes and glazes of color if you want to retain the pitcher's form.

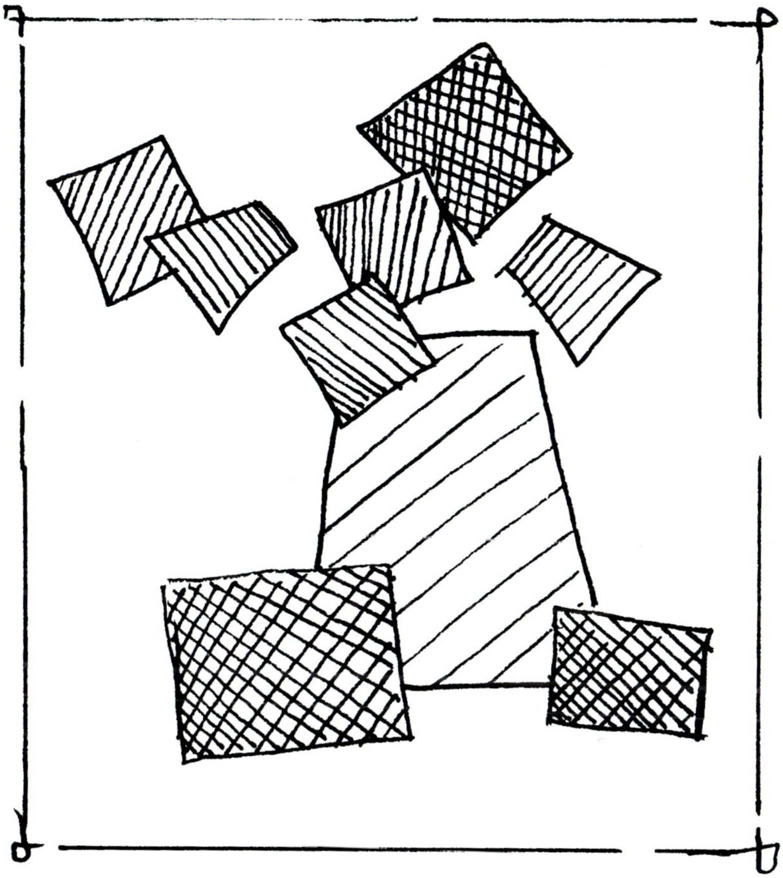

◀ **Planning the Composition** When you look at the shapes in the photo reference all together, they suggest a grouped mass. This sketch shows that for the strongest composition, a few minor adjustments are necessary—such as moving the smaller pumpkin to the left so it overlaps the pitcher.

"As practice makes perfect, I cannot but make progress; each drawing one makes, each study one paints, is a step forward."
–Vincent van Gogh

Underpainting and Negative Shapes Just as in the daisy demonstration, using an underpainting here establishes a toned surface for the flowers and the area behind the pitcher.

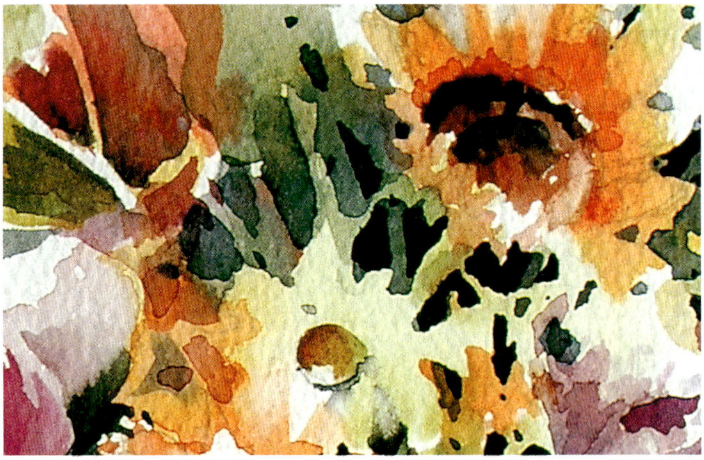

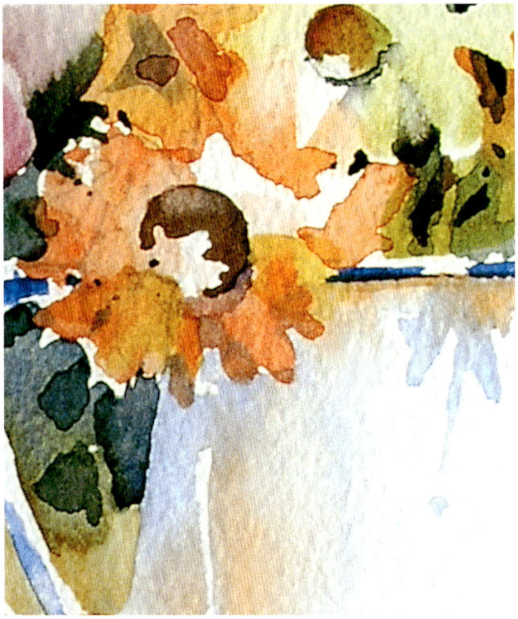

Reflected Light Reflected light helps define the pitcher, preventing it from looking flat and unnatural. The form shadows are alive with blues from the background and oranges from the pumpkin and flowers.

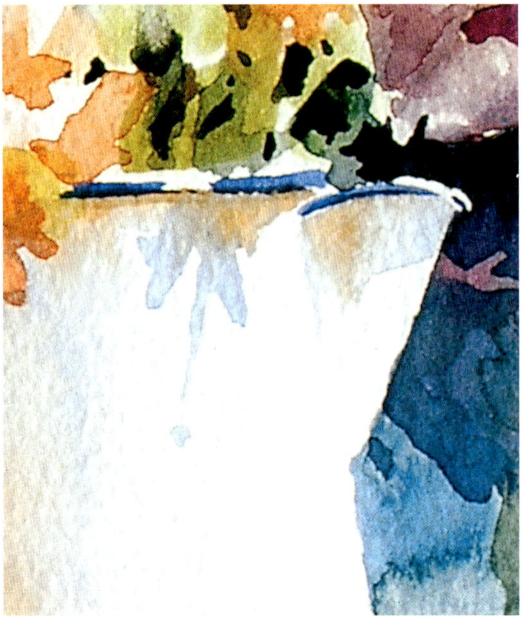

Glowing Whites The final touch is setting up a strong contrast. Place the white pitcher against glowing, rich darks to define its shape and make it really stand out. The deep blue works well because it complements the orange of the pumpkins.

If you have "lost" some of the precious whites of your painting, don't panic! Lifting out color is still an option (see page 12)—just be sure to wait until the end of the painting process; once the surface of the paper is disturbed, it will not accept paint smoothly again.

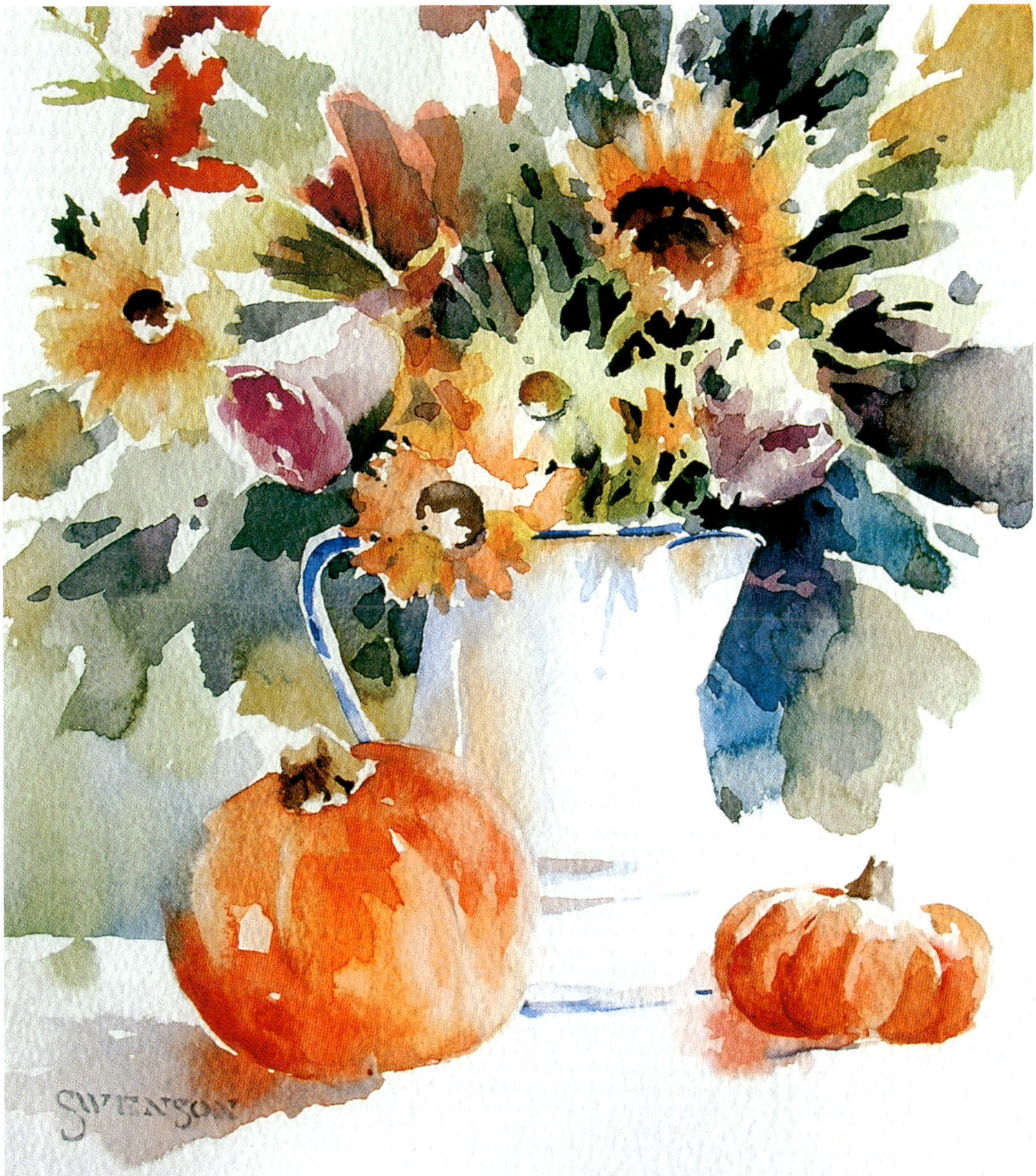

Although most of the flowers in this composition aren't white, you can still paint the majority of them with negative painting. (Negative painting isn't reserved just for whites—you can use this technique to define any lighter value areas.) The pitcher almost paints itself! All you need to do is paint a form shadow on the left side, adding some color reflected from the pumpkin. On the right side, near the spout, apply a dark value of blue to contrast with the white.

Put It All Together

In each lesson, you've focused on one essential preparatory painting step. But in reality, none of these steps can exist separately—each and every step is influenced by the others, and you must combine them all to create a successful watercolor painting. Here you'll see how it's done, step by step, with a demonstration that takes into account everything you've learned up until now. Success is within reach—it's just a matter of putting it all together to create your own wonderful finished work!

Considering the Subject Never begin a painting without first asking yourself, "What do I want to say?" This helps you determine what is most important, allowing you to eliminate any unnecessary information. The white house in the foreground asserts itself as the obvious center of interest here.

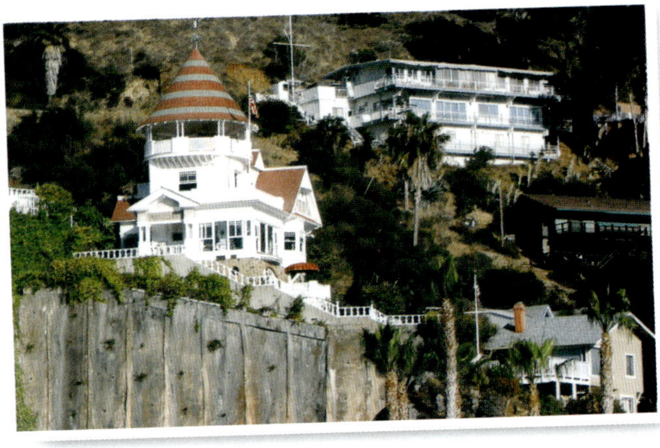

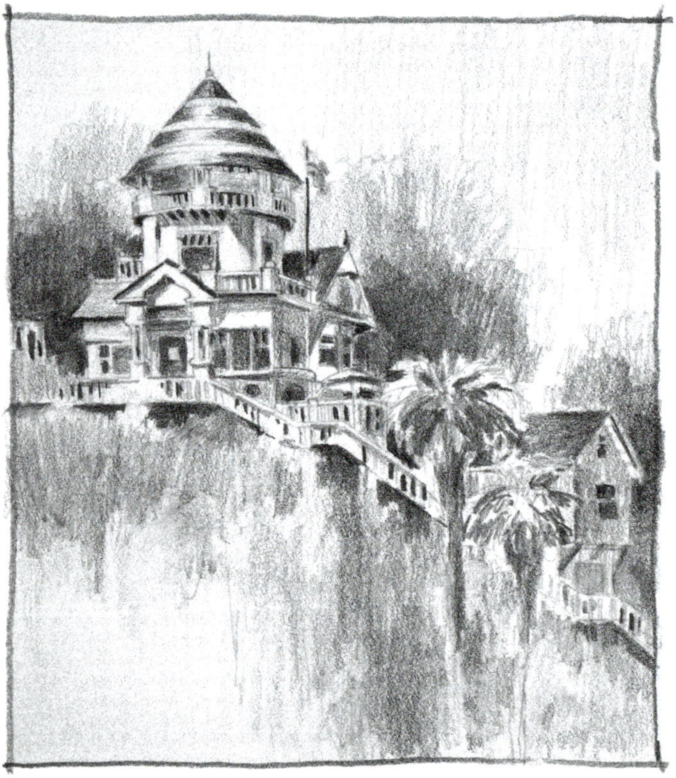

Planning the Design You may find it helpful to work out your value study and design plan at the same time. Removing the hill (along with the distracting background houses) helps showcase the subject. And adding foliage in front of the building directs the eye into the composition and adds color. The cruciform design naturally suggests itself.

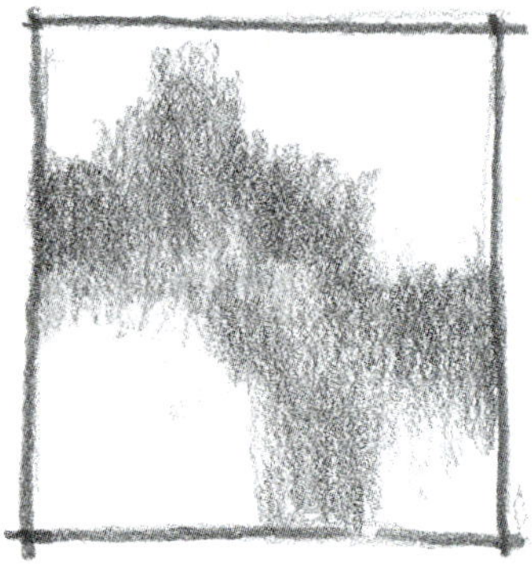

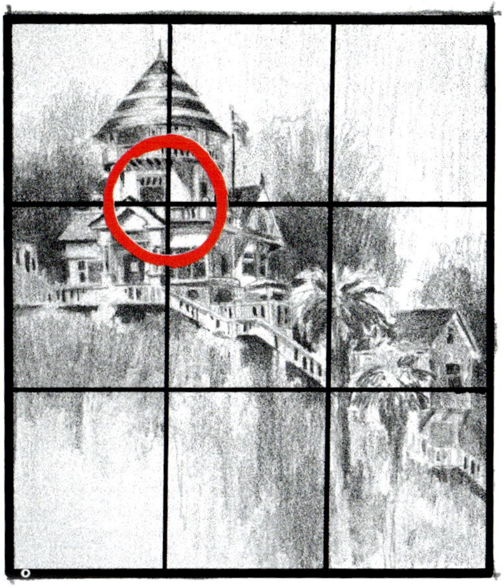

◀ **Checking the Plan** Keep the intersection of thirds in mind when you place the focal point of this scene. The focal point here is the building—but more specifically, it's the front entryway. Does the grid hit the target exactly? No, but it's close enough!

▶ **Starting with a Sketch** Every successful watercolor painting begins with a sketch. Before you can learn to paint well, you must first learn to draw. How else can you ensure that the proportions and perspective of your image are realistic representations?

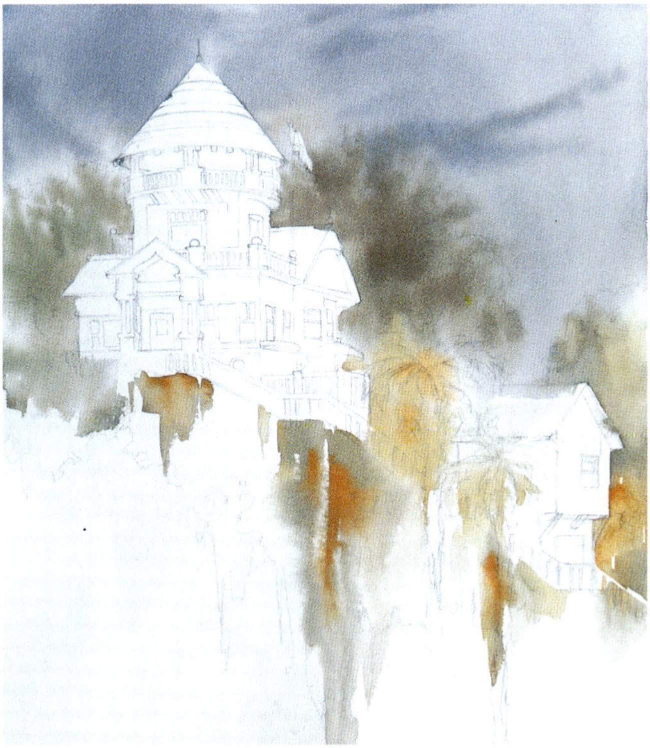

Step One Here the focus is on value, color, and edges. Eliminating a lot of the unnecessary whites early on will help you better gauge the values in the painting. After wetting the sky and the area below the house, apply a gray mix of complementary permanent carmine and cupric green deep to the sky. For the trees, mix cupric green deep with burnt sienna, adding raw sienna to the mix for the outer edges. Timing is critical, as you want soft edges between the sky and trees. Now pull the tree colors into the area below the house, introducing a bit of permanent orange into the wash.

Step Two Shadows and glowing whites are important now. There are form shadows on the dome and on the building where it turns from the light, and there are cast shadows on the front of the building. Link as many shadows as possible together to keep the painting from looking choppy. Approach the building shadows by first painting a passage of cobalt blue, then adding a touch of permanent orange before the blue dries. Warm autumn colors will be placed below the building, so be sure to reflect them in the shadows.

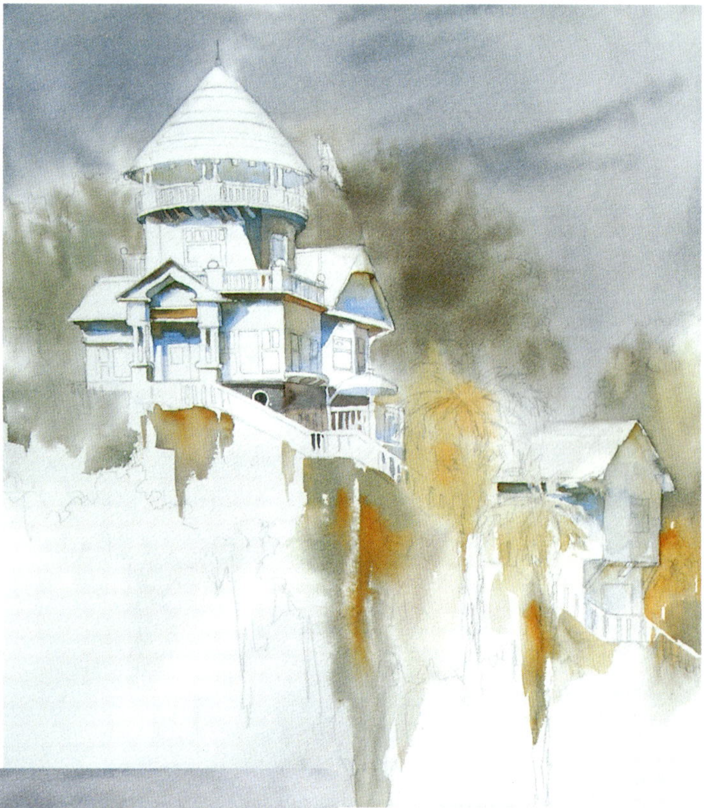

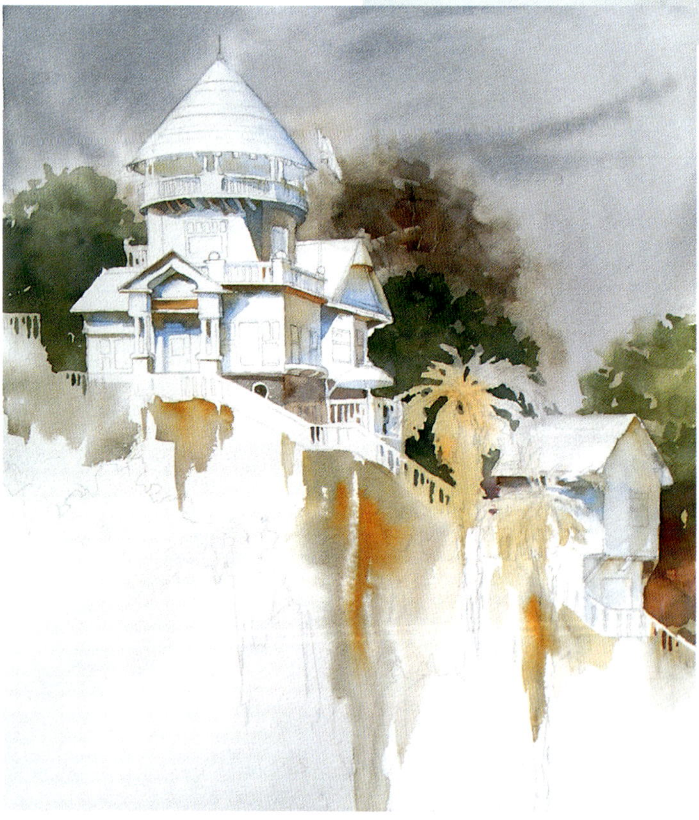

Step Three The focus now turns to negative painting. At this stage, place the majority of the trees with a mix of burnt sienna and marine blue. To tone down the green in the right corner, I also apply a bit of scarlet lake. Painting the trees fills in the negative space that is defining the overall shape of the house. The dark values behind the house help the building stand out. Use the same tree color mix to define the white railing and the top of the palm tree, again painting negatively to define the lighter-valued objects.

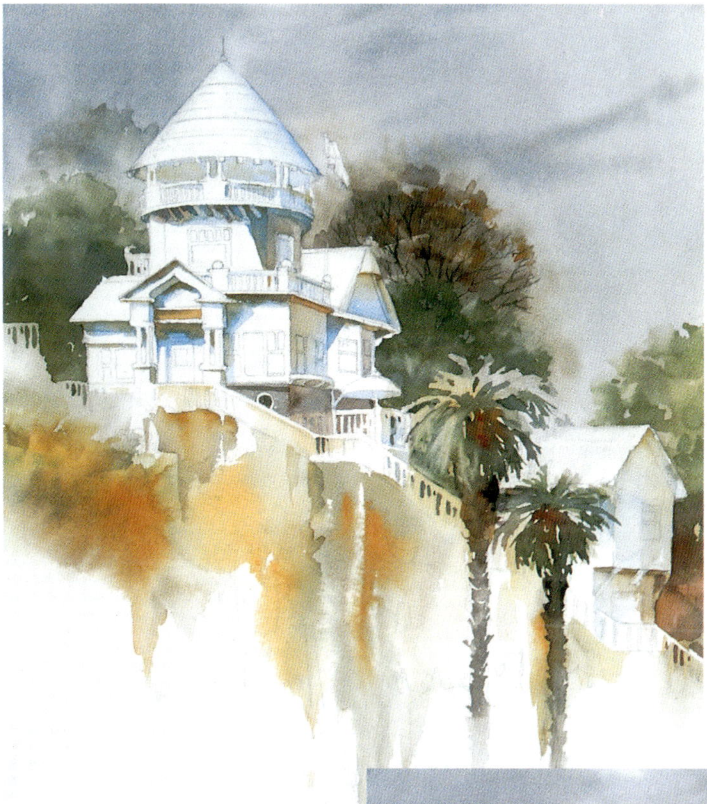

Step Four Design is crucial here. The palms are important—they complete the cruciform! Paint them with the tree mix from step three, adding burnt sienna for the trunks and scarlet lake in the centers of the palm fronds. Moisten the paper below the house on the left before applying a mix of permanent orange, new gamboge, and a touch of burnt sienna. Use the same mixture to paint the tree at the right of the house, defining its branches.

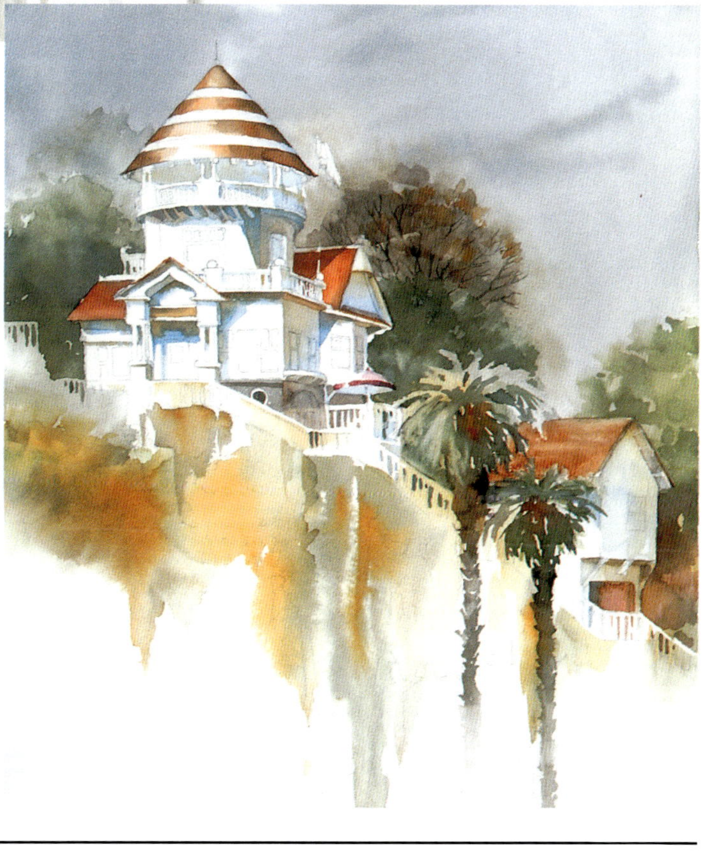

Step Five Now form shadows are the main focus. For the rooftops and dome, apply burnt sienna mixed with a touch of scarlet lake. The value isn't consistent all the way around the curved dome—it has form shadows and highlights. Place lighter values where the dome comes forward and darker values where it recedes. Paint around the highlight where the light is striking the dome directly. Note that the rooftop on the right contains a cast shadow from a taller part of the building.

Step Six The center of interest and color are the keys to this step. Although the front entryway is the focus, the red striped dome draws the eye, causing the dome to become too dominant. To neutralize the red, glaze over the dome with the gray sky mix (which contains green). To liven up the wall below the house, apply granulating colors lunar black and manganese blue hue, allowing them to mix on the paper.

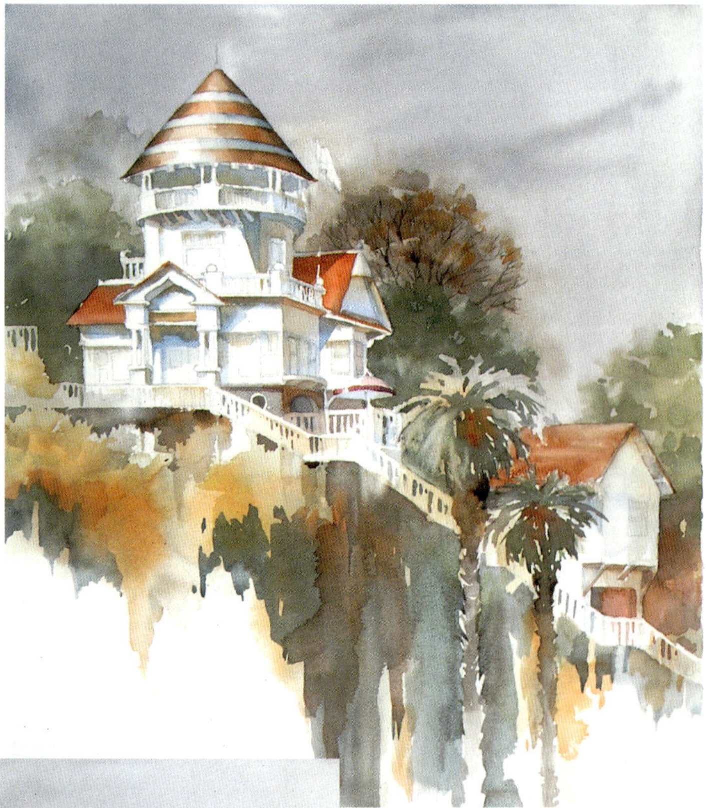

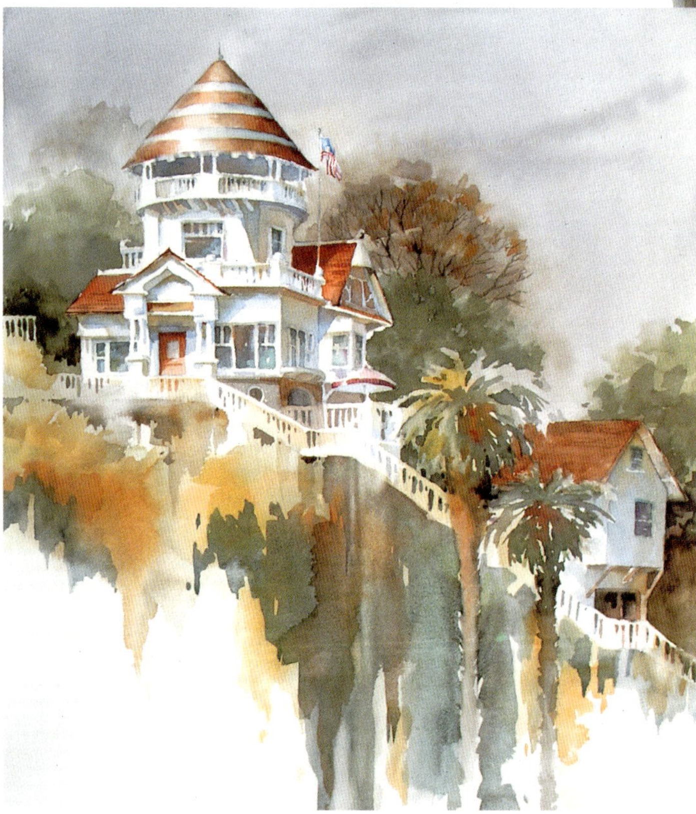

Step Seven At this stage, the center of interest, values, edges, shadows, and negative shapes all demand attention; you'll make value adjustments, soften edges, and add details. Paint the front door red with a cast shadow across it. Then adjust the form shadows on the building's right and under the dome, glazing cobalt blue mixed with permanent orange. The scarlet lake added in step three is attracting too much attention, but you can lift out the color at this stage to adjust and restore balance. Finally, add a flag for interest.

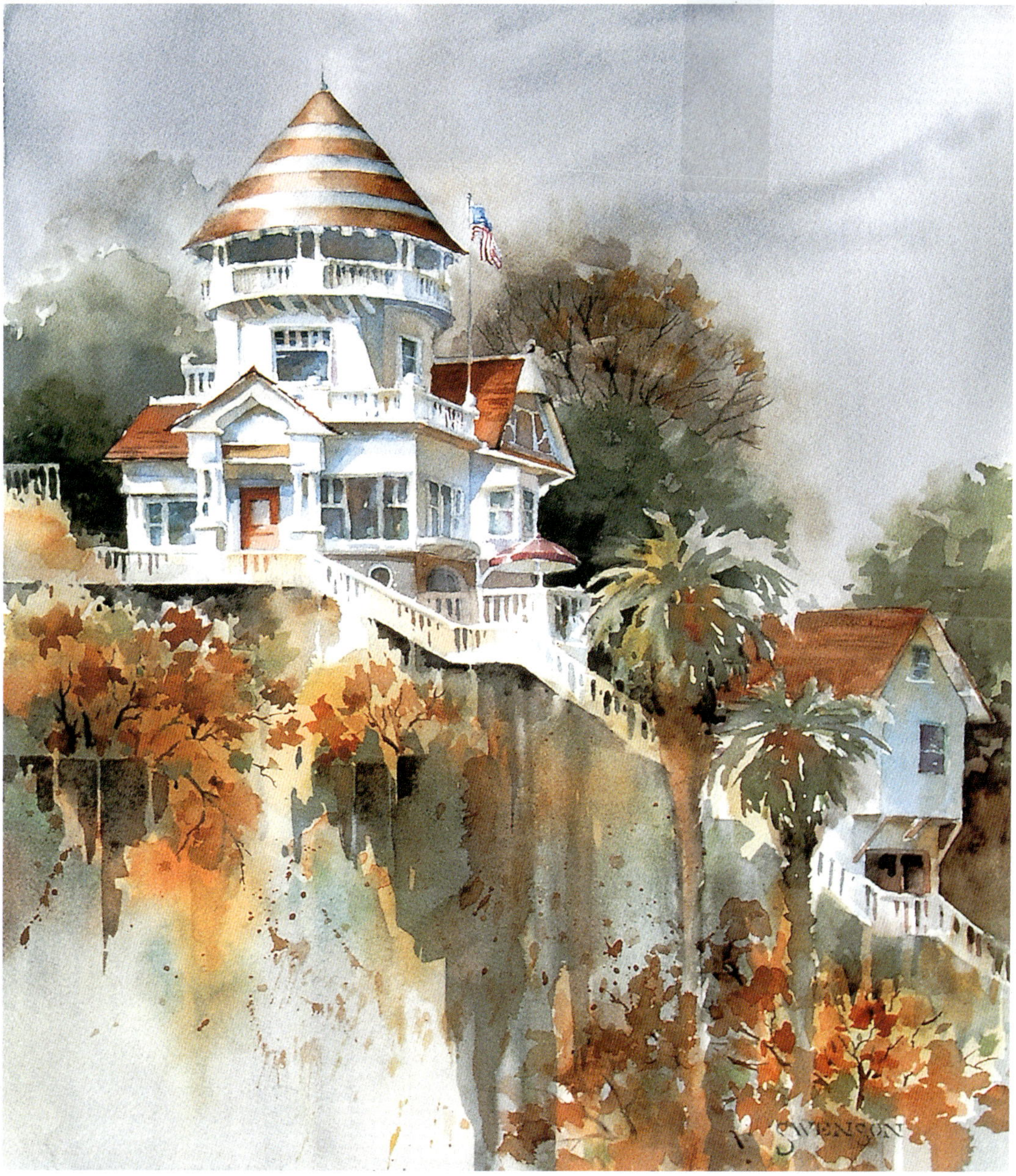

Step Eight Now it's time to think more and paint less! You're nearly done—you just need to make a few final tweaks to balance out the values. Put down your brush and scrutinize the painting. The lower left corner appears barren in comparison with the rest of the painting; for balance, add a light wash of granulating lunar black and manganese blue hue. Next suggest foliage with warm burnt sienna and quinacridone sienna. Once again, darken the green directly behind the house on both sides, strengthening the contrast to make the white stand out. Then the painting is complete!

The Learning Curve

Watercolor is an unpredictable medium, which makes it uniquely challenging. When I first began painting, everything felt so unfamiliar and awkward in my hands. Fortunately, my fascination with watercolor was stronger than my frustration. In a short period of time, I became comfortable with the paper, brushes, paint, and water-to-paint ratios. Before I knew it, I was making great strides with this challenging medium. I was on my way!

And then something happened. I felt like everything I spent so long learning was unfamiliar again. What was going on? I can't tell you why this happens, but I can reassure you that the feeling of distress will pass. My own experiences have taught me again and again that during these periods of struggle, the greatest amount of learning and growth is occurring!

Why am I telling you this? The last thing I want you to do is give up! With each new skill you learn, a new challenge will present itself. But as the climb becomes more difficult, the rewards become richer. So keep painting—and keep challenging yourself to take your work to the next level and beyond!

Happy Painting!
Brenda Swenson

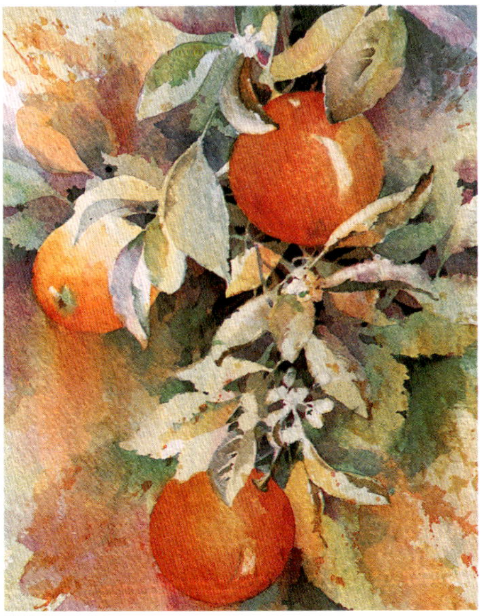

"There are no days in life so memorable as those which vibrate to some stroke of the imagination."
—Ralph Waldo Emerson